<small>ADVANCE PRAISE FOR</small>

The Awakened Dreamer

"Kala Ambrose is a beautiful force of nature, exploring many fascinating realms. In *The Awakened Dreamer* she gives us access to and understanding of the world of dreams. When one considers we spend a third of our lives asleep, this is a tremendous gift indeed. From getting a good night's sleep to learning to master dreams by taking control in lucid dreaming, Kala is a masterful guide through Morpheus' territory."

—Maureen Seaberg, *Psychology Today*

"Are you ready to create a deeper spiritual and psychic connection through your dreams? Then we suggest letting Kala Ambrose be your guide… A powerful intuitive, Kala teaches you how to remember and interpret your dreams, how to use daydreams to manifest your personal dreams, and how to communicate with loved ones and spirit guides on the other side through your dreams."

—Amy Zerner and Monte Farber, authors of
The Enchanted Tarot and *Karma Cards*

"Kala has a poetic gift of sharing her wisdom in a way that weaves you into a world of spiritual awakening through everyday tips. *The Awakened Dreamer* offers the same practical guidance as her other riveting books, but specifically related to your dreams and better understanding why they matter. What you dream, why and when can be applied to your life in ways you never imagined. She offers insights on how to interpret your dreams, [how to] get better at remembering them, and how you can incorporate what you learn to shed old patterns, bring you peace about a situation, or help you through a trying time in your life."

—Renee Blodgett, managing editor
and founder of *We Blog the World*

The Awakened Dreamer

About the Author

Kala Ambrose is a modern muse and your travel guide to the other side. Renowned intuitive coach, podcaster, and lifestyle expert, she helps entrepreneurs and visionaries live their best lives. Kala's books and online courses are described as empowering by thousands worldwide who have been inspired by her teachings. The award-winning author of six books, including *The Awakened Psychic*, *The Awakened Dreamer*, and *The Awakened Aura*, she shares how to connect with your soul path in order to create a life and career that is in tune with your life purpose and goals. Study online with Kala through her school, the Academy of Mystical Arts and Spiritual Sciences, at Explore YourSpirit.com.

HOW TO REMEMBER & INTERPRET
YOUR DREAMS

The Awakened Dreamer

Kala Ambrose

Llewellyn Publications
Woodbury, Minnesota

FIRST EDITION
First Printing, 2017

Cover design by Cassie Kanzenbach

Llewellyn Publications is a registered trademark of Llewellyn Worldwide Ltd.

Library of Congress Cataloging-in-Publication Data
Names: Ambrose, Kala, author.
Title: The awakened dreamer : how to remember & interpret your dreams / Kala Ambrose.
Description: First Edition. | Woodbury : Llewellyn Worldwide, Ltd., 2017. | Includes bibliographical references.
Identifiers: LCCN 2017033315 (print) | LCCN 2017043156 (ebook) | ISBN 9780738754062 (ebook) | ISBN 9780738753119 (alk. paper)
Subjects: LCSH: Dreams.
Classification: LCC BF1091 (ebook) | LCC BF1091 .A4925 2017 (print) | DDC 154.6/3—dc23
LC record available at https://lccn.loc.gov/2017033315

Llewellyn Worldwide Ltd. does not participate in, endorse, or have any authority or responsibility concerning private business transactions between our authors and the public.

All mail addressed to the author is forwarded, but the publisher cannot, unless specifically instructed by the author, give out an address or phone number.

Any Internet references contained in this work are current at publication time, but the publisher cannot guarantee that a specific location will continue to be maintained. Please refer to the publisher's website for links to authors' websites and other sources.

Llewellyn Publications
A Division of Llewellyn Worldwide Ltd.
2143 Wooddale Drive
Woodbury, MN 55125-2989
www.llewellyn.com

Printed in the United States of America

Other Books by Kala Ambrose

The Awakened Aura:
Experiencing the Evolution of Your Energy Body

The Awakened Psychic:
What You Need to Know to Develop Your Psychic Abilities

Ghosthunting North Carolina

9 Life Altering Lessons:
Secrets of the Mystery Schools Unveiled

Spirits of New Orleans:
Voodoo Curses, Vampire Legends, and Cities of the Dead

Dedicated to all the dreamers, big thinkers, and visionaries out there. You know who you are and you know when you dream big, there's no limit to what can be accomplished.

Dream on!

Contents

Introduction

EXPLORING THE POWER OF YOUR DREAMS

What if I told you that you had a magical power that has always been available to you and that you had been ignoring it your entire life? That this ability is something every person experiences every day within a twenty-four-hour period, whether they want to or not?

I'm talking about dreams, of course, something we all experience. Many people will tell you that they don't dream; however, science has proven that this is not the case. What is factual is that some people don't remember their dreams. Sleep studies have shown that the average person experiences a dream around every one and a half hours of sleep during a regular sleep cycle.

Throughout history, dreams have been recorded by people from a variety of cultures and groups who profess to have had dreams that warned them of danger, storms, wars, death threats, infidelities, betrayals, illnesses, and, at times, better days to come.

In modern times, the Western world has pushed aside the intuitive abilities of dreams and of listening to that voice within, in a sense silencing and creating a disconnect from the soul.

Like all good things, however, the secrets of the soul cannot be fully contained, and the power of dreams is being resurrected, researched, and even studied by scientific types to the amusement of mystics, who have always known how magical and informative dreams can be. Many historians have long agreed with psychologists that dreams can tell the future and that they are indeed a form of divination. Some religious scholars share these traditions as well.

In my book *The Awakened Aura*, I share how dreams were used in the healing process in some ancient temples in order to help healers diagnose the deeper issue ongoing in the mind-body-spirit connection to treating disease. The understanding was that what you think and feel contributes to a feeling of unease in the body, which can over time manifest into a physical ailment. While you could just treat the physical ailment, it made better sense to get to the root of the problem and treat that as well, so that the ailment would not reappear in the body. The healer would watch over the patient as they slept, paying attention to when they were dreaming and taking notes. When the patient awoke, the doctor would ask them about their dream in order to interpret what was causing stress in this person's life.

Some of these dream temples became hugely popular, including the temple of Asklepios in the ancient Greek city of Pergamon, in modern-day Turkey. People traveled to this site to ask for assistance and answers to their problems through their dreams. While this temple conducted a more formal process in order to receive this type of divination, people in many other cultures worked with shamans or priestesses or even communed with their deceased ancestors in dreamtime in order to receive guidance and answers to their daily problems.

Wise women and men still seek guidance through their dreams today. There are reports of people who have a dream about an illness and then seek medical treatment for this ailment before experiencing any outward physical signs of any problem. In addition to these reports, a wide variety of entrepreneurs have shared with me that most of the innovative ideas that led to their success came to them first in a dream. When we ask for answers to a problem or for a fresh idea, many times the response is sent to us through a dream. When we can remember our dreams and then know how to interpret them, we open a new door of communication to the universe that can lead to a wellspring of inspiration, ideas, and guidance.

One of the most fascinating aspects of dreaming is when you have dreams about yourself in which you are acting out of character. Perhaps in the dream you are acting bolder and more assertive, taking risks that you wouldn't normally. This type of dream I often call "the stirring of the soul," coming from your higher self or superconscious mind, encouraging you to be brave and to try new things. This often occurs first in our dreams so that we can try it out and see how it feels, preparing our conscious mind for this new adventure. For many of us, our dreams are our first steps in embracing change in our lives.

When I work with someone to help interpret their dream, a good portion of my time is spent pulling out as many details as I can from their dream. Once I have the list of details, I then review with the client what each of these symbols and scenarios can potentially mean. Next, I ask the client what specific meaning and feelings are attached to these particular items. Through this process, together we are able to achieve the deepest understanding of what the dream was attempting to communicate from the subconscious to the conscious mind. By following the steps laid out in this book, you will learn how to create your own dream research notebook along with the steps for how to analyze and discern the meaning of your dreams.

In my school, the Academy of Mystical Arts and Spiritual Sciences (AMASS), I share with my students the difference between the arts and sciences. Dream interpretation is a bit of both, as there is a scientific aspect that can help analyze the dream. But the scientific view can only take you so far in this work. The art of dream interpretation is where the best results are achieved.

This is discovered by practice and by looking at dreams for years, for yourself and for others if you choose. Over time you'll discover a baseline for what dreams mean for you and what they are saying. Intuition, in order to see what the symbols are hinting at, also plays a big part in dream interpretation, as does psychic ability, to receive deeper spiritual information that may be coming from spiritual guides in the dreams that I describe as teaching dreams or prophetic dreams.

A Lifetime of Awakened Dreaming

At this point, I trust that I've intrigued you enough to want to explore what your dreams are telling you. First, though, I should back up for a minute and explain a little bit about how I came to write this book.

My name is Kala Ambrose, and I'm known as your travel guide to the other side. I'm a psychic medium, a wisdom teacher, and the author of six books, including *The Awakened Aura, The Awakened Psychic,* and the one you're reading now, *The Awakened Dreamer.*

All my life I have seen and read auras as well as experienced prophetic dreams, communicated with ghosts and spirits, and seen what's going on psychically with people in their past, present, and future. I came back in this lifetime remembering my past lives and being able to explain these previous lives to my parents. I've dedicated this lifetime to the study of comparative religion and philosophies, including ancient wisdom teachings from Eastern and Western cultures, and I'm an astrologer, dream interpreter, numerologist, tarot reader, and traditional feng shui practitioner. I've worked with scientific research institutions to study paranormal abilities, and I've taught around the United States at prestigious centers. As a psychic and wisdom teacher, I teach entrepreneur intuition, in which I coach my clients on how to see future trends in order to grow their business or career. In my online school, AMASS, I teach students around the world how to develop their psychic ability, how to see auras, how to use their intuition to build the business of their dreams, and how to interpret and manifest their dreams.

My life has been dedicated to this work, and I share and teach through my books, my school, my podcasts, my blog, and any other opportunity given to me. It's my great joy to awaken people to the possibilities that are available to them through their spiritual connection. In this book, that's just what I'm going to do as your guide. Throughout this journey, I will show you how to remember your dreams, how to interpret them, and how to use daydreams to manifest your wishes into reality.

With this information in mind, it's important to pay attention to your dreams, no matter how young or old you are or how unrealistic they may seem. I learned this valuable lesson at a very young age, somewhere between six and eight years old, when I had a prophetic dream that someone was going to break through the gate attached to the fence in my family's backyard and steal our little dog.

When I woke up from this dream, I was upset and began to cry. It took me a moment to realize that it was just a dream, as it felt so real and so final. While I knew that this dream was as real to me as anything that occurred in my daily life, I didn't quite know how to explain how profound my dreams were to me at that time.

Distraught from the dream, I ran from my bedroom to find my parents at the kitchen table, where they were enjoying breakfast. Tears still dampened my cheeks as I flung myself into my father's arms and told him and my mother about my dream. They listened attentively and consoled me, explaining that it was just a bad dream.

"No," I insisted. "It's real. It's going to happen." I begged them to let our dog sleep in my room with me. My mother and father empathized with how the dream was making me feel but stood strong on their decision that the dog would not be sleeping in my room. Back in those days, many people with pets did not bring them into the home; they were outside dogs only, and our dog was not allowed in the house.

Taking my feelings into consideration, they took the time to comfort me and explain why my bad dream was just that.

They shared with me that they were saying no for the following reasons:

- We lived in a relatively small town, and there was little crime in the area and virtually no crime to speak of in our neighborhood, especially a crime like dognapping.
- My father was a police officer and was well known and liked in our community. The chances of someone coming to our home to break down a gate were highly unlikely.
- Our sweet dog, while cute as could be, was a mutt. There was no value of a pedigree that might entice someone to take the dog and sell him for a profit.

My parents' explanation made sense, but I insisted on the accuracy of my dream. Again I pleaded with them, explaining that this event was going to happen this evening. At the core of my being, I just knew it to be true. I begged them to allow the dog to sleep in my room. Weary of my story and of my begging, they firmly said no and sent me to my room to get ready for school.

That evening I was anxious, and at bedtime I begged my parents one last time for permission to have the dog sleep in my room. They said no and wished me a good night with pleasant dreams this evening.

I fell into a fitful sleep that night and woke early the next morning. I rushed outside to check on our dog, only to find the gate broken and our dog gone, just as the dream had foretold.

Running back inside our home, I woke my parents with my sobbing. "I told you this would happen," I said inconsolably. "Why wouldn't you listen to me?"

My father had been called away during the night for work, and he was still a bit foggy headed that morning from little sleep. He tried to calm me and said that perhaps I was mistaken and had awoken from another dream.

"No," I assured him, "I went outside to see." He looked down to see me wearing his boots. I had pulled them on before running outside, as I loved to wear his boots and his police shirt around the house.

By this time my mother had put on her robe, and the three of us went outside into the backyard, where I showed them the gate, which had been broken in the exact manner that I had described in my dream.

He and my mother were completely shocked. At the time, I remember thinking that the surprised look on their faces was just about my dream being true. Now as an adult I realize that, while they found the coincidence of my dream to be surprising, they were more concerned that someone had been on our property during the night while my father was away and that they had taken the time to break open this sturdy gate. Perhaps they stole the dog, or perhaps the dog ran away during this event. He had slipped through the gate a few times before and loved to run, which is why the gate had been fortified and secured in order to keep him from escaping again.

I wish I could say that they believed me after I told them about what I called my "real" dreams, which is how I described the dreams I had that felt like they were part of real life and not the fuzzy, random dreams that we all have otherwise. However, they weren't quite ready to believe in my dreams. Several years later when I had a dream of such tremendous detail regarding what would occur with the passing of a family member, they were forced to accept that, like it or not, my "real" dreams were predictions of the future.

This experience also awakened my scientific side and my love of paranormal research. I had been seeing ghosts and spirits for as long as I could remember, but they rarely did anything that was even remotely scary or mean. The most frightening aspect of them that I could recall was just the surprise when they appeared, as you weren't expecting to see someone in the room, and there they were.

As a psychic and someone who had prophetic dreams (ones that come true), I was aware that the information provided in psychic glimpses and dreams wasn't always the clearest. It was like glimpsing images and part of the puzzle but not seeing the event from start to finish. The psychic clues provided in the dream gave me an idea of what had occurred, but they didn't spell it out from start to finish. I could sympathize with my father and his fellow detectives as they worked a case from their perspective, having only a few clues to work with, to figure out what had occurred and if it would happen again. This dream about my sweet dog prompted me to start my first dream journal and my first psychic hunch journal, which I've continued throughout my lifetime.

Years later as an adult, I went to my mother and begged her to tell me what she truly knew about what had happened to our little dog. I explained that as an adult I would understand whatever had happened and that it still haunted me to this day that I could not stop it from happening. She told me that she truly had no idea what had happened that night.

Many years later, I had a dream of my dog in doggie heaven, and he said he would come back to me again one day when I was an adult. I never expected to have a dog at this point in my adult life, but this prediction came true, and the dog I have now has the exact same characteristics and personality of my dog in childhood, even though they are two very different breeds. Coincidence? I prefer to think not.

It was during this time that my intuitive skills began to flourish. I was coming into my own and understanding that my dreams and the intuitive flashes I had when awake were both showing me things that others could not see. After that first major dream experience, I began to hone my ability to remember my dreams and to discern what they were trying to communicate with me.

Over this lifetime, I've become an expert dreamer, learning how to lucid dream, how to distinguish prophetic dreams from everyday dreams, and how to use my dreams to help manifest what I wish to achieve in my life. For several decades now, I've been teaching people specific techniques on how to pay attention to their dreams, how to interpret their dreams, and how to manifest their dreams. The results have been amazing, and I continue to hear from my students and clients as I teach online and in person how remembering their dreams has changed their lives and how learning to understand and work with their dreams has empowered them, well, beyond their wildest dreams.

This book is a guide to learn how to do all these things while also inspiring you to dream big. Together we'll explore how to discern what your dreams are telling you so that you can understand their language and take action on what they are showing you.

One

How to Remember Your Dreams

Everyone dreams nightly, whether they remember their dreams or not. You can learn how to remember your dreams and, even more importantly, how to interpret what they are telling you.

My dreams have been very helpful and important to me, and I pay great attention to them. They have guided me in decision-making, have connected me with loved ones on the other side, have warned me about problems to come, and have been an amazing source of inspiration and creativity.

I've consciously remembered my dreams since childhood and can on almost any given day recall at least three dreams from the previous night in vivid detail. Over the years, I've classified my dreams into four categories:

Daily Life Dreams: I dream about things on my mind and in my subconscious that I am working through in my daily life. This type of dream allows us to work through troubling events and personal experiences that we are unsure how to handle on an emotional level. Daily life dreams include random and strange dreams that make little sense at the time, as our emotions are processing these feelings through our subconscious.

Prophetic Dreams: I intuitively dream about people, places, and events to come.

Teaching Dreams: My higher self journeys to the other side to explore and learn.

Visitation Dreams: Loved ones and guides in spirit visit me.

As an intuitive, dream interpreter, and wisdom teacher, I teach about the incredible value in interpreting and manifesting your dreams and share with my students how to evaluate what their dreams mean. This includes showing them how to take action on dreams that warn of danger, how to discern what each dream is trying to communicate, and how to become a "lucid dreamer," consciously aware that you are in a dream state and able to alter the dream at will.

Our dreams connect us with our higher self in the spirit world. It is possible to receive direct guidance through our dreams, and we can communicate with our loved ones and spirit guides on the other side through our dreams. We can activate this connection to pursue a deeper spiritual and psychic connection. Additionally, we can also harness this ability to enhance our daily living in many ways, including getting a more restful and peaceful night's sleep and sharpening our focus and mental acuity.

In this book, I'll teach you how to remember your dreams, how to interpret them, how to communicate with those in spirit, how to discern prophetic dreams, and how to take your dreams and turn them into guided visualizations in order to help you connect with and manifest your wishes and desires.

Together we'll explore how to connect your subconscious desires with your conscious dreams in order to awaken to your divine state as a conscious creator and awakened dreamer. You'll learn how to live in this state of connection and grace, where each dream can lead you to new opportunities, unleashing your creativity.

Exercise: Techniques for Peaceful Sleep and Creative Dreams

Interpreting your dreams is not as difficult as you may believe. You have the wisdom, and as your travel guide to the other side, I'll walk you through each step to tuning in to your dreams. Over the years, I've developed a series of techniques for achieving the highest potential in my dream state, including learning how to achieve lucid states in dreaming, in which I am consciously aware of my dreams and can actively enter each dream and change the situation at will if I so choose. I also have kept a dream journal for decades so that I can analyze dreams and look back on them to see what they were telling me in great detail. With this practice, I have become very skilled at dream interpretation, not just for myself, but for others as well.

First, though, to be a good dreamer, you have to be able to relax and sleep well. With this practice, I have created a series of techniques that allow you to connect with your higher consciousness through your dreams while achieving a restful night's sleep.

Step 1: Create a Soothing Environment

The area where you sleep should be as clutter free and peaceful as possible. Make sure you have plenty of soft and warm covers to curl up in and pillows that allow you to rest comfortably. Pajamas should be loose and made of cotton if possible, as cotton is a natural fiber that allows energy to flow. Synthetic materials can block energy flow as well as trap your body's ability to sweat and breathe.

We sleep better in a cooler environment, so lower the temperature on the air-conditioning in the summer in order to ensure that the room is nice and cool. Aromatherapy can also be helpful to relax your mind and body before drifting off to sleep. Many people use aromatherapy in the bedroom, spraying a lavender-chamomile or a lavender-vanilla pillow mist such as the type sold in bath and body stores that can be safely applied to sheets and pillowcases. I've even seen sleep masks that contain a hint of lavender inside of them. What's most important is that you are comfortable and relaxed. Where you sleep should be as tranquil and supportive as possible.

The colors of your bedding and decor, including artwork and soft lighting, should be given great thought. Does the room invite you to relax and drift peacefully to sleep?

There's a hotel that I love that has a Bose sound system next to the bed and provides a selection of music that is relaxing and inviting. When you check into the hotel and enter your room, this music is playing, and it's a most welcoming feature. It immediately puts me in a good mood and I relax, thinking, *Okay, I'm here and the vacation begins.* Many times at night when I'm trying to unwind and get ready for sleep, I think of my favorite song from the list and picture myself lying on the bed in the resort. Hearing the song in my mind instantly relaxes me and brings a smile to my face. Create little rituals like this in your bedroom that are soothing and relaxing.

Step 2: Nightly Preparations

When possible, conduct your nightly bedtime routines at least a half hour before you decide to go to sleep. This includes showering, brushing your teeth, applying moisturizer, picking out clothes for the next day, doing laundry, or anything that might wake you up a bit with the activity. Give yourself these thirty minutes before bedtime to just relax in your pajamas and unwind. Try not to watch TV or engage in any stimulating conversation before you prepare for bed, as the movie or show may play back in your mind when you sleep, influencing your dreams.

My husband and I created a routine in which anything that we needed to discuss, such as plans for the next day and decisions about things going on in our lives and in the household, were all discussed after dinner and several hours before we went to bed. This allowed us to make plans as needed but also spend time together each evening before bedtime just relaxing and enjoying the evening, rather than having potentially stressful discussions right before trying to go to sleep.

It is helpful to avoid drinking caffeine at least three hours before going to sleep. This should go without saying, but also avoid drinking alcohol on a day when you want to work on remembering your dreams that night. Alcohol, many prescription medications, and other drugs can affect and influence your dreams in ways that make them unclear and unreliable. When under the influence of some drugs, mind-altering effects can occur and can cause hallucinations or nightmares. When under the influence of alcohol, the rapid eye movement (REM) stages of sleep are affected, which can lead to disturbing dreams that are not truly connected to the emotional state of the person.

If you are taking any prescription medication, ask your physician if these medicines are known to affect sleeping patterns and dreams. Many people have asked me if one glass of wine is enough alcohol to affect your dreams. For most people, one glass of wine at dinner will not have an effect, as it is mostly absorbed with the meal, but several glasses of wine and wine later in the evening are usually enough to affect the clarity of your dreams. If you have imbibed an amount that will affect your dreams, a good indication is feeling buzzed or a bit numb after drinking. One glass of wine doesn't have much of an effect on me, especially with a meal, but three glasses of wine do have a clear effect on my system.

As a person who can see auras, I can clearly see when someone has been drinking or when they are taking narcotics or prescription drugs. It used to amaze my husband how clearly I could see it. A person would walk into a room and I could tell him that the person had a drink of alcohol not too long ago. He would go ask them and they would confirm that they had just had a beer or other alcoholic beverage. In the aura, the energy field around the body, there is an immediate and easy-to-see reaction when we drink any type of alcohol or take any type of drug or medication. When you want to do any type of spiritual work, including connecting deeper with your dreams, you want your body and energy field to be as clear and unencumbered as possible.

Last, on an evening when you want to explore astral travel or have a deeper connection with the spirit world in your dreams, refrain from eating a heavy meal for dinner, such as steak or other hearty meat products. A lighter meal of chicken or vegetables is easier and quicker to digest before bedtime. It is also helpful to eat dinner three to four hours before going to sleep and to avoid late-night snacking or at least limit the snack to something light eaten no later than a hour before bedtime.

Step 3: Surround Yourself in Pure White Light

Each night before preparing to sleep, visualize being surrounded by a cocoon of peaceful, loving energy and white light. See this light forming an oval around your body, protecting you in a beautiful and warm force field of energy that nourishes and protects your body while you sleep. This ritual can become a daily practice that not only nurtures you, but also raises the energy field in your aura. As you create the light around you, state out loud that you are surrounded by the pure white light and that only your highest and best can be made manifest through to you.

As you visualize this pure white light surrounding you, see the light glow in incandescent colors as it moves around your body. The light is warm and peaceful and loving and comforts you. You are relaxed and safe.

If you like, you can expand this white-light energy so that your bedroom is filled with this soft white light. The light clears any old energy from the room and makes it purified and clear, filled only with the energy of love, protection, and goodness. Nothing else can penetrate this loving field of energy.

As you practice this ritual of surrounding yourself and your room in the beautiful white light, in the future you can expand this to surround your entire home in the white light. See it growing bigger and traveling room by room in your home. In each room that it enters, it removes any old energy and transforms the room into a peaceful and loving space. The light fills your entire home and expands outside of your home, creating a peaceful white-light shield and bubble that surrounds you and everyone inside in a cocoon of light and love.

Sleep well, knowing that you have transformed your home that evening, filling it with peace, love, and harmony, which will allow everyone sleeping under your roof to enjoy a good night's sleep. This is a wonderful ritual to do every night, regardless of whether or not you want to focus on your dreams, as it brings comfort to everyone.

Step 4: Breathe and Release

Now that you are in bed and have surrounded your area in the beautiful pure white light, it's time to prepare for dreamtime. Take three deep breaths in and out to relax. Breathe in deeply to the count of three, hold the breath for a count of three, and then release the breath in a count of three.

During each breath cycle, visualize clear, cool, pure, positive white-light energy coming into your body as you inhale. When holding the breath, imagine this beautiful energy circulating throughout your body, and as you exhale, see any negative thoughts or emotions that you were holding on to inside being released as you blow the breath from your body. This negative energy is released from you. It drifts away and dissipates into nothingness. Because you have also created the white-light bubble in your room, as you release old energy, the white light accepts this energy and quickly removes it from the room.

Not only are you preparing yourself for good dreams, but you are also doing ancient healing techniques that are removing negative toxic thoughts and energy from your mind, body, and spirit, clearing and cleansing all your energy fields. This helps your body relax and your thoughts and emotions be open to releasing any stress from the day.

After taking the three deep breaths, find the position that is most comfortable for you to sleep. Focus first on your toes. Wiggle your toes and then in your thoughts remind them to relax. Then gently flex your feet forward and back and remind them to relax. Work your way up through your ankles, your calves, your thighs, and your hips, gently moving them and reminding them to relax. Continue up your body, reminding your solar plexus area to relax, and as you reach the heart and lung area, take another deep breath, visualize all stress leaving your body, and relax. Raise your shoulders, slightly bringing them closer to your head, and then as you bring them back down, take a deep breath and release, letting all the tension from your shoulders melt away. Wiggle your hands and fingers like you did with your toes and feet, and remind them to relax. Gently rotate your head in a clockwise motion, with a final reminder to your entire body that you are relaxed and ready to dream. At this point, you should be feeling pretty good.

Step 5: Forgiveness on a Divine Level

In this relaxed state, allow your mind to peacefully review the events of your day. If there was an unpleasant encounter that pops up into your thoughts, immediately catch this thought and notice how your body has tensed. Take a deep breath, stop the thought, and release the stress and tension with your next outward breath. Breathe deeply and relax the areas of your body that have become tense with this thought. Then ask your higher self to see this experience with compassion and greater understanding from all perspectives.

You are now focusing on seeing this experience without the immediate emotional reaction connected to your personal feelings. In this moment, you are seeing the experience from a detached view so that you can see how everyone was affected during that event. Focus on breathing deeply as you review this event in your mind. Let the tension of the experience be released from your body with each breath you exhale, knowing that the pure white light around you is absorbing this energy and dissolving it so that it no longer creates tension in your body.

While reviewing this situation, if you find that you did something that you now regret, resolve to take positive action on this matter as soon as possible. If it is within your ability to apologize to the person the next day, make plans to do so, so that you can let this matter go for the time being this evening.

If you are not able to reach this person directly, picture them in your mind at this moment. As you see their image, speak directly to them, asking for their forgiveness and apologizing for your actions. This allows for a clear conscience on which to drift peacefully to sleep.

In essence, when you picture their image in your mind, you are speaking to their higher self, the part of each of our souls that resides in the higher planes of the spirit world. In this practice, you are reaching out from your soul to theirs, asking for forgiveness that may not be easily attainable in the human form at this time.

Step 6: Guided Meditation

Now that you have surrounded your body in protective and peaceful white light and have let go of any negative energy stored in your body as well as any troubling thoughts or concerns, you have purified your body and energetic space and are ready to fall into a deep and empowering sleep. In order to set the tone for your dreams, begin with a guided meditation.

You can make up a meditation of your own choosing or listen to a guided meditation that is recorded. This meditation should put you in a happy and peaceful place, perhaps focusing on relaxing the body or going to a place you love in nature. The meditation doesn't have to be long; a few minutes will do the trick. If you make up one of your own, it can be as simple as imagining yourself in a place that you love and where you feel happy and relaxed.

One of my favorite meditations that I create before drifting off to sleep is to picture this beautiful old English-style house with a big formal library filled with books. In this gorgeous library, there is a very large window that looks out to the English garden outside filled with lush flowers. The colors of the flowers are pink and green and yellow and blue and red. The big window that looks out to the garden has a wonderful window seat with a deep soft green velvet cushion and big pillows nestled against the sidewalls. I enter the library, and on the desk there is always a new book that has been picked out for me, awaiting my attention. I pick up the hardback book—the cover varies in color from deep blue to forest green to burgundy red—and I settle into the window seat on the green velvet cushion. Lying back against the pillows there, I take a deep breath, gaze out the window for a moment to view the gorgeous flowers outside, and often find that a gentle rain is coming down outside. After a moment of gazing into the garden, I draw my attention back into the room and open up the book in my hands. As I begin to read the first page of the book, I say in my thoughts, *This book contains the information that I need to dream about this evening.* At this point, I'm pretty relaxed and drift off to sleep, in a space that is ready and receptive to my dreams.

If meditation doesn't work with you, consider a sound machine that plays the gentle sounds of nature like rain or the ocean.

Now you're ready to drift off peacefully to sleep, and it's time to enter dreamtime.

Exercise: Training Your Mind to Remember Your Dreams

Once you have created a bedtime routine for positive sleep cycles, it's time to begin training your mind to remember your dreams.

Step 1: Peaceful Sleep

Begin with the six steps for techniques for peaceful sleep and creative dreams, starting on page 14.

Step 2: Set the Intention

Say out loud to your mind that each night before you go to sleep, you will remember your dreams when you awake. Setting this intention each night will train your mind that this is an activity that you wish for it to do.

Step 3: Record Your Dreams

Keep a notebook or voice recorder and a small flashlight by your bedside table so that each time you wake during the night, you can record or jot down notes about your dreams.

At first, this will feel awkward and may upset your ability to return back to sleep right away. In time, though, you will be accustomed to this activity and that it will become so normal that you'll wake and be able to jot these thoughts down and fall right back to sleep.

When you first begin this work, you probably won't remember the entire dream. You'll remember bits and pieces of the dream or maybe just the last part of the dream that occurred when you woke up. This is completely normal. Eventually, you will move from remembering bits and pieces of the dream, to remembering sections of the dream, and finally to remembering the entire dream.

If writing down the dream feels too complicated at first, try drawing a simple picture of what the dream looked like with a few descriptive words. This is why it's helpful to have a pen and paper. An example is drawing a simple picture of your home, but in the dream it looked different because the house was by a river and you were standing outside with your grandfather looking at some flowers. Draw a simple house and write "my house," put some waves in the back and write "river," and draw two stick figures and label them "me" and "grandpa." These simple descriptions will be enough to help jog your memory about this dream.

Step 4: Record Your Emotions

Record how you felt when you awoke from this dream. Did you feel happy, peaceful, scared, anxious, or excited?

Write down a word that describes how you felt in the dream. This will also help you interpret the dream in the future.

Over time, you will notice that some symbols repeat themselves in your dreams. Take notice of these symbols and record them in your journal, as they will help you more quickly analyze and interpret your dreams in the future.

Step 5: Scheduling and Timing

When first learning how to remember and record your dreams, you can try it for a few nights a week, like on a weekend, when you can sleep in longer in the morning. Over time, you'll be able to do this anytime you'd like.

Set your alarm clock to a sound that begins softly and then gradually gets louder until you finally turn it off. The soft sound and gradual awakening, rather than a loud burst of noise, will help ease you from sleep, allowing you to remember your dream and to write it down first thing in the morning. When you awake, remain in your current position and slowly reach over to grab your dream journal and pen. Lie in bed and write down everything you can remember. It's better to do this than to hop out of bed. When we take physical action, the mind jumps to being aware of what we are actively doing, which can cause it to focus on our physical activity and let the dream slip away.

If you have an evening when you are not worried about your sleep cycle and can catch up on sleep the next day, you may wish to experiment with setting your alarm clock to go off every one and a half to two hours throughout the night, as this is about the cycle of each time you drift into sleep and dream. To do this, you may want to sleep alone in a private room so that you don't disturb your partner sleeping next to you.

Each time the alarm goes off, ask yourself what you were dreaming, write down what you remember, set the alarm again for another hour and a half to two hours, and try again. If you were having a dream that you were interested in, state before going back to sleep that you'd like to return to the dream you were having and experience it in greater detail. We'll talk more about this and lucid dreaming in future chapters.

Creating New Sleep Cycles

When you are ready to go to the mastery level of dreaming, you may wish to consider altering your sleep cycle in a new direction, which may be different from what you were told were normal sleep patterns.

On evenings when I wish to actively engage with my dreams, I create a sleep pattern that lasts for several hours as I enter an active dream state. I set the intention with my higher conscious self, telling it before I go to sleep that I want to be woken up each time I have received beneficial and useful information through my dreams. Think of it as setting an internal alarm clock that your higher self is operating.

At the end of each dream cycle, which for me lasts around three hours of sleep, my higher conscious self awakens me from my dream state. As I awake, I am usually filled with an abundance of creative ideas, and my thinking is much clearer than it was before I went to sleep. I usually rise at this time, write down the dreams, and work on projects like writing my books for an hour or two. Once this creative energy is released, my body relaxes, and I go back to bed for another sleep cycle of three hours. By conditioning myself to be open to this type of sleep cycle, I am able to receive the information through my subconscious and higher consciousness and work effectively in interpreting the dreams and visions received during this time.

This type of sleep cycle is effective not only during nighttime sleep, but also for naps during the day. Before taking the nap or going to sleep for the first sleep cycle, state the intention to your higher consciousness that you are now going to sleep and that you wish for the sleep cycle to be restful, rejuvenating, and full of information that will be useful to the work you are focused on at hand. Also state that when you have experienced these dreams, you would like to be awakened so that you can write them down and release the creative ideas and energy.

I have found that this sleep and dream cycle works well for me, as I wake rested and energized each day. I still sleep eight hours each day, but it is in two or sometimes three different sleep cycles. This pattern is something that I engage in when I am involved in a creative project for a period of time like writing a book. It's a joy to be able to engage in this type of sleep cycle, which is now possible with my work as a writer, as I can set my own schedule. Other times, I do adhere to the typical eight-hours-straight sleep schedule when I need to be engaged in work that revolves around the current corporate style of nine-to-five for conducting business.

I've taught this technique for years in workshops and explained how this type of sleep cycle can be very invigorating, and I have shared information and research that states that a straight-through eight-hour sleep cycle may not work best for some types of people. I share how visionaries including Thomas Edison, Nikola Tesla, Thomas Jefferson, Sir Isaac Newton, Leonardo da Vinci, Napoleon Bonaparte, Benjamin Franklin, and many other artists, inventors, visionaries, and entrepreneurs have reportedly used this same sleep cycle.

Recent studies on sleep patterns and cycles were conducted in order to determine whether the recommendation of an uninterrupted eight-hour period of sleep is indeed the best advice. According to a 2012 BBC News report, studies on historic and scientific data are now revealing that the uninterrupted eight-hour sleep cycle may be an unnatural cycle that we were not intended to follow. The report shares that in the past in many cultures, humans slept for three to four hours, then got up for a while, and then returned later to sleep again. Many people toss and turn at night, unable to get a straight eight hours of sleep, and feel more stressed as their mind and body are unable to relax. As a result, they resort to prescription drugs to sleep, which can cause more disruptions to the body over time. This does not allow them to come to terms with the stress that is causing their discomfort, nor does it allow them to experience and discern what their dreams are attempting to communicate to them.

Following the techniques for peaceful sleep may allow for more restful periods of sleep as the mind has let go of the problems, turning them over to the higher consciousness to work on creative solutions. In this practice, the emotional concerns have been addressed by either resolving to take action in person the next day or to apologize through mindful visualization in order to neutralize the conflict and allow a person's thoughts and emotions to return to a relaxed state.

I'm not a doctor or psychiatrist, and this is not meant to be advice in any way; it's just a practice that I and others have used that works well for us in our work as entrepreneurs and artists. I share this technique here, as some people may wish to see if it works for them. What is most important is to get a good night's sleep, in whatever capacity works best, and that differs for each person. Good sleep equals good dream opportunities and options.

Exercise: Generate Creative Ideas through Napping

Many of the visionaries listed previously believed in the creative power of naps in order to problem-solve throughout the day. I agree 100 percent and have adopted the practice they used, which appears to have been used for hundreds of years. Here's how it works:

When you are ready to take a nap, sit comfortably in a chair instead of lying down. In your hand, hold an object that is not too heavy, fits comfortably in your hand, and is noisy, making a loud sound when it is dropped onto the floor. I use a small ball made of copper, which makes a loud noise when it drops onto my hardwood floor, for this exercise.

Once you have selected this object and placed it in your hand, allow your arm to rest on the arm of the chair with the hand extending outward toward the floor in a comfortable position. Relax in the chair, visualize the white light around you, and take three deep breaths in and out. Then set the intention to your mind and higher self that you are attempting to find a creative solution to the problem at hand that you have not considered before and that as you take this nap, a solution will be presented to you through your dreams.

Now drift off to sleep and take your nap. Because you have set the intention that this particular nap is to focus your higher self to engage with all the creative ideas that exist in the global consciousness and to present this information in your dreams, the information will come very quickly. This is a good thing because, remember, you are holding an object in your hand. As you fall further into sleep, your hand will eventually relax and the object will drop and hit the floor, awakening you by the sound it makes. When you awake, focus on remembering what you were dreaming about, as many times the answer you are looking for is there in the dream.

If you can't get used to the Old World idea of holding an object, a modern technique is to set your smartphone alarm to fifteen minutes. With this exercise, typically the answer comes within fifteen to twenty minutes or not at all. If it doesn't work during a nap, don't give up—that evening set the intention again for a solution to come in your dreams.

Bad Dreams: The Dreams We Don't Want to Remember

We all have bad dreams. Some are so terrible we wake up with our heart racing and in a cold sweat and panic. It's a relief when we realize that it was a dream and not actually occurring in the moment. However, the problem as an awakened dreamer and burgeoning dream interpreter is discerning what is a prophetic dream and what isn't.

Remember the tips about how alcohol, drugs, and eating too close to bedtime can affect your dreams? It's also important to note that some bad dreams occur when we are ill or feverish. If you have a cold, fever, or upset stomach, disregard the dreams that come through, as they are too difficult to discern and usually too convoluted to understand clearly. The majority of bad dreams not caused by these circumstances are usually what I described earlier as daily life dreams, in which you are working out a problem or concern in your life on the subconscious level. These dreams are trying to help you release stress and worry and and engaging you to consider how to take action on the situation as well as how to deal with your fears. Write these dreams down in your journal so that when your head is clearer, you can review this information and determine what your subconscious mind is trying to explain.

When you wake up from a bad dream, take a deep breath and blow it away, visualizing the bad dream leaving you and dissipating into nothing. Then shake your head: literally give your head a gentle shake, as if to reset and reprogram your mind.

As you prepare to go back to sleep, announce that you intend to only have good dreams this evening and do not wish to be disturbed by any dreams except for good ones.

As we delve deeper into this book, we'll explore what to do about the bad dreams that are prophetic and are warning you about an event to come.

In Review

At this point, you have some homework to do—start teaching yourself how to be a good sleeper and a good dreamer. Look at the descriptions you've been jotting down each day in your journal. In the beginning, it's helpful to use this journal every day, as the information is fresh in your mind and you can add more detail and information before the dream dissipates, as it often does. Dating each of the dreams will assist you in beginning to predict timing in dreams as well as help track which dreams you have that come true.

Like all things in life, the more you practice, the better and easier it will become. You'll also discover which sleeping patterns work best for you to remember dreams.

This practice will help you in future chapters when I discuss how to "daydream" when you're awake to get this information, so start now so that you're ready to move on to even greater things.

Two

INTERPRETING YOUR DAILY LIFE DREAMS

Now that you are sleeping well, remember your dreams, and have created a notebook or journal, it's time to start interpreting what your dreams are telling you.

In this chapter, most of the dreams we will discuss fall into the category of the daily life dreams. At first glance, when reviewing dreams, some of them can seem pretty easy to figure out, like a dream about being scared of something that you're afraid of in real life. But in dream interpretation, there are many levels below the surface that must also be considered.

With the ability to interpret your dreams, you can connect the bridge between the subconscious, the conscious, and the superconscious mind and work through situations in your life very quickly through dreamtime.

To explain further, the subconscious mind is hidden. It records every thought, feeling, and action we take, but it often hides this information from the conscious mind. Though it is hidden, it influences the conscious mind, often leaving us wondering why we feel a certain way about something when it makes no logical sense to our conscious mind.

The conscious mind is the active part of the mind with which we make all our daily decisions and take action. It is very busy but is often reactionary and unaware of our deeper thoughts and feelings.

The superconscious mind is what I also refer to in the spiritual sense as the higher self, the part that I see as connected to our soul. The superconscious mind is aware of everything that is happening to us in our human body on the earth, while also being connected to the spiritual planes of existence.

While we have a conscious, there is also a "global consciousness" that holds all the thoughts and ideas of all humanity above the earth plane. Our superconscious can access this fount of ideas and often does. This is where we pull great ideas "out of thin air" or where they come to us "out of the blue." In my book *The Awakened Aura*, I describe this as the aura, the energetic field around the body, which is able to reach into the global consciousness and the higher spiritual planes to connect with these masterful ideas and thoughts as well as seek guidance from spirit guides to help with decisions and life plans.

When we meditate or when we learn how to engage directly with our dreams and our daydreams, we can access the superconscious and gain greater insight to and inspiration from what our dreams are attempting to communicate to us.

In your dream journal, you are writing a brief description of each dream along with how you felt emotionally in the dream. As you remember more about your dreams, the descriptions become more vivid and detailed. You've also begun to note symbols that repeat frequently in your dreams. In the appendix, I discuss the most common dream symbols that people experience, so you can flip back and forth as needed to help interpret the symbols in your dreams. Keep in mind, though, that these are suggested definitions for common symbols and may not always be the case. The best interpreter of your dreams is always going to be you because you understand on a much greater level what is going on in your daily life.

As you become more skilled at recording and interpreting your dreams, you'll begin to see the patterns that appear in your dreams.

Let's look at two example dreams that will give clues on how to interpret a dream.

Dream Example 1: Banana Dream

Imagine that you have a dream about a banana that follows you around in dreams that have to do with your love life. This banana is always interjecting its thoughts about what you are doing in your dreams whenever you dream about being with a lover, whether that person is from your past, present, or perhaps future.

If you were to look up online or in a book what this banana might mean, you might read that bananas are a fruit and that dreaming about fruit usually indicates happiness. You might also find specifically that bananas are a reference to a penis, and so this can indicate that a new loving partner who will bring you romance and sexual pleasure is coming into your life.

On a personal level, when interpreting the rest of the dream, including why the banana follows you around and is giving you advice, you may recall upon further reflection that your great aunt was named Anna and that your great uncle and everyone else always called her Anna Banana. Anna Banana loved to give advice about relationships and was known as a great matchmaker. She is coming to you in this dream in the form of a banana so that you will distinctly remember what she is saying. Most people remember a talking banana when it appears in their dreams more than they remember a relative.

When you look back at your banana dreams at this point, you can see clearly how the talking banana was indeed your great aunt, whether she was communicating with you from the spirit world or whether she was just a representation that your higher conscious self used to help you work through your thoughts about your relationships.

Let's say that in one particular banana dream, you were in a café where you had just broken up with your last relationship partner. As you left the café, this giant banana was standing outside and began to follow you. The banana would not stop talking about how you always pick the wrong type of partner and why you were never satisfied.

These are the first indications of what the dream about the banana is attempting to communicate to you. Here's what you do to interpret your dreams:

Step 1: Become Aware of Your Emotions and How Actively You Are Participating in the Dream

The first step when interpreting your dreams is to determine how you felt emotionally in the dream. Were you experiencing a strong emotion, like fear or joy, or were you more of an observer in the dream, watching the event unfold without feeling an emotional connection?

In the example of the banana dream, you were actively engaged in this dream, having just broken up with your most recent lover. As you left the café, you felt sad, wondering if you would ever find someone who truly understood you and whom you felt could be a real partner in your life. The banana kept you company as you processed these feelings.

As you think about the meaning of this dream, you realize that you long for a relationship with a person that you are also friends and partners with in life, with a deep spiritual connection. In addition to these attributes, you want to be romanced and to experience passion in this relationship, with intense and fulfilling lovemaking.

Step 2: Determine What Subliminal Message Was Shared with You in the Dream

In the banana dream, did you feel relieved that this relationship was over? Perhaps while the breakup was difficult, it was a restrictive and unsatisfying relationship that wasn't working for you.

Thinking back to the banana now, was the talking banana sad like you, or was it upbeat, reminding you that the love you are seeking will soon find you?

What message did you receive now that you can think back on the dream?

Step 3: Determine the Subject of the Dream

Looking back at your notes from your dream, determine whether the dream was directly about you or a story about other people.

For example, in the banana dream, the focus is about you. The banana is talking, but it's giving you advice about what just occurred with your breakup and what relationship may come for you in the future. The person you broke up with in the dream plays a very small role in the dream: they are there and they are gone, and the rest of the dream is focused on your feelings about what you deeply want in a relationship with someone new.

Determining whether a dream is about you or about someone else is very important, especially when it comes to predicting prophetic dreams.

Step 4: Consider the Frequency of the Dream

If the dream is about you directly, it's important to look over your notes about what happened to you in the dream and compare them to how you felt emotionally.

If this dream repeats itself, you are being prompted to take active steps to work through this problem. The dream is attempting to show you what is on your subconscious mind.

In the case of the banana dream, the dreamer is being shown that they are ready to pursue a relationship that will meet their needs and expectations on the mind-body-spirit level and that it's time to seek out a partner who is looking for the same experience.

If you want to take your dream skills to the mastery level of dream manifestation, when reviewing your dream the next day, state out loud that you are ready to meet the right person for your next relationship. Ask the universe to show you this person when you meet them by having a banana somehow appear around them as a sign. Perhaps you'll meet this person in the break room at work eating a banana or in a grocery store with bananas in their cart, or perhaps during a conversation when meeting someone new, somehow the word "banana" is mentioned or referenced.

Dream Example 2: Falling Dream

Let's look at another type of dream to interpret. For example, let's say you had a dream that you were falling, which is a very common dream.

Since you are having the experience of falling, this dream is about you directly. Perhaps you see the cliff that you fell from or a tall building, and now you are falling and feeling the wind rush around you.

Step 1: Note How the Dream Feels

Are you falling quickly, or is the fall in slow motion, taking up most of the dream? Are you scared, or are you looking at your surroundings as you fall, such as the windows in the building or the balconies or a tree growing sideways off the cliff? Do you see people in the windows as you fall past the building? Is someone hanging onto a tree branch and reaching out to catch you?

All of these details are important as you process the emotional temperature of how you felt in this dream.

If you are falling in slow motion and observing your surroundings, this can mean that you are aware of a potential "fall or pitfall experience" coming into your life. If you are able to observe your surroundings in this dream, you will be consciously aware that there are opportunities to receive help during this experience, which will help stop your fall. In this case, you could reach out to grab the balcony to stop your fall, or the person in the tree branches may reach out to catch you along the way.

If you are falling quickly and feeling afraid, it can mean that the experience that is coming will catch you unaware and off guard when it happens. The surprise of it will temporarily make you feel that there is nothing that can be done to help. This is your subconscious and higher conscious self trying to warn you the best they can that an unexpected surprise of an unwelcome nature is coming your way.

When having a dream like this, it's a good reminder to have a little pep talk with yourself that you are strong and can handle what comes your way, even when it comes as a surprise. The surprise might take you off guard for a moment, but there are always resources available to help you.

Once you are able to move past the first instinct of fear in this type of dream, look past your emotions into understanding what the dream is communicating to you in more detail.

Step 2: Look at the Color and Size of Objects in Your Dream

What color was the building, the sky, the tree limb? What color clothing were you wearing?

All of these colors indicate the challenge around you and how ready you are for the experience to come. If the colors are vibrant, you are at full strength and will easily bounce back. If the colors are more muted, they may indicate that there will be a greater emotional trauma through the experience. In this particular dream, the colors in the sky will be the most telling, as will the clothing you are wearing.

The next aspect to note is the size of things in your dream. How tall is the building or cliff? How large are the tree limbs or the balconies on the building? If the limb is very large and substantial, it indicates that help will be within easy reach. The same is true if the balcony is of ample size. If the branch or balcony is small, it means that help will be available, but the majority of the work will come from you.

Step 3: Note the Length of the Dream

Do you fall for most of the dream, so that you are falling for so long that even in the dream you start to wonder what's happening?

This is describing the amount of time that the experience will take. If it's a very long fall, it can indicate that the situation will go on for some time. If the event leading up to the fall takes a long time (say, for example, you are standing up at the top of the building for a long time or at the edge of the cliff for an extended period), it indicates that there will be clues to what is coming and you have time to prepare.

Step 4: Determine the Subject of the Dream

At this point we've discussed what it means if you are the one falling in the dream. What does it mean, though, if you are not the one falling? What if instead you are dreaming about other people or objects falling from the sky?

When it's not about you, it's usually about watching an object or objects fall rather than other people. The focus is on the object, the type of object, and the number falling.

The best way to interpret this is to consider rain. If raindrops are intermittently falling, you are aware of it, but it might not stop you from your activity. You might hasten to finish your work before the rain falls more heavily, but the drops are manageable. However, if the rain is pouring down around you, all work stops and you seek shelter. This is the same with objects falling. If one object is falling from the sky in your dream, take notice and determine how large it is, how close it is to you, and how quickly it is falling. Is the object falling over a forest, a city, or a specific area or space that you recognize?

All of these are clues to how the object will affect you or others. If there are many similar objects falling at the same time, this gives warning that what is to come will be more intense, like a thunderstorm rather than a gentle rain shower.

The Most Common Types of Dreams and What They Mean

There are dreams that are so common that almost everyone can share a story of having a dream of this type. Most of them fall into the daily life dream category.

Chasing Dreams

In dreams in which you are being chased, many times you never see what is chasing you; you just experience the fear of being chased and needing to run or hide.

It is most important in these dreams to note what action you take. Do you run and run and keep on running, or do you seek shelter and hide? If you hide, is there a familiar place you seem to return to frequently?

In general, chasing dreams typically indicate that you are running away from something, such as a problem, a person, or both combined. If you can see who or what is chasing you, it can help identify the problem. For example, if your mother is chasing you in the dream, it can indicate a problem with her directly, or it can indicate that you are not not dealing with something to do with your feminine side.

Other clues should be considered in the dream as well as what's going on in your personal life. If a woman is having this dream, the next question is, are you a mother or thinking about becoming a mother, and if so, are you concerned about how you will be as a mother in comparison to how you were mothered?

If the being chasing you is an animal, it's important to note the type of animal. Is it the proverbial wolf at the door? Or when you finally can turn around in this dream and confront what is chasing you, perhaps you find that the wolf changes into a gentle lamb, which has been trying all this time to help you soften and connect with your emotions regarding this particular situation.

In coming chapters, you'll learn how to interact with your dreams while dreaming so that you can engage with the characters in your dreams and change your dreams at will.

Falling Dreams

A great majority of people have indicated having a falling dream at least once in their life. As described earlier, the dream is connected with a feeling of loss of control in a situation.

Flying Dreams

Many dreams that begin with falling move into flying. This can be associated with facing a fear and realizing that not only can you handle this situation, but you can be free from the fear and master the situation.

When flying, notice how you fly and where you are flying. Is it over a city or so high in the sky you can only see the clouds? How do you fly—is it Superman style, with your arms stretched out in front of you, or are your arms out to the side like a plane? Do you move around while flying—are you able to do flips or veer left or right? How about hovering—can you float stationary in the sky and look around? Do you leave Earth's atmosphere and fly into space?

The more control you appear to have when flying, the stronger you are feeling about your situation. Flying dreams are almost always about feeling free in some way and reaching new heights.

Magical Power Dreams

The most fun common dream is having magical powers! This is always a good sign, as it indicates that you are connecting your subconscious mind with your conscious and superconscious minds and are realizing your unique gifts and abilities.

It means that you are awakening to understanding how to achieve what you wish for in your dreams and life goals. Pay attention to what magical power you have been given in the dream and see how you can harness this symbolic power in your daily life.

The only time this dream is negative is when you dream that you can't do something and wish you had a secret magical power to make it happen. This indicates that you are not connected with your personal power and believe that you can't make something happen on your own.

Money Dreams

Money dreams can involve winning money, finding money, earning lots of money, or losing lots of money. That's no surprise, as money dictates so much of what goes in our lives and in the modern world: money is necessary for survival, to give us shelter, nourishment, and care.

Most money dreams really don't indicate that you are winning or losing money. If you want a sign that you are about to come into money, I still say that the itching palm is the best indication. This is an Old World teaching that I have found really works. When your left palm itches, it means money is coming to you from a source outside of yourself, such as winning a lottery or an inheritance or gift. When your right palm itches, it means money is coming to you from your hard work, in the form of a raise or promotion.

So then what do money dreams mean? If you are winning money in your dream, it indicates general success in your endeavors, from which you will prosper. If you are losing money in the dream, you are experiencing lack of self-confidence and are in doubt about the situation at hand. If you are losing a lot of money or dream about having lost all your money, you are concerned that you do not know where you belong or what your status is in life.

These types of dreams happen often when experiencing a loss, such as losing a loved one, going through a divorce, moving, changing or losing a job, and other big life changes. While it's easy to see how in any of these scenarios money is a potential problem, the dream is actually related to how one feels about the situation and if they have the potential to prosper and move forward.

What surprises many people is that dreams about money often indicate thoughts and attitudes about love. A person who dreams about being generous and wanting to share money with others or give it away is a person who is very loving and looking to share their love with others, so it can often indicate a new relationship is coming. On the other end, a person hoarding and withholding money or feeling like they never have enough money in a dream feels unloved and insecure. They are hoarding because they feel that they are not truly being cared for and loved by others.

A combination of the two, in which you are giving away lots of money and feel that money is slipping away too quickly, can indicate that you are giving too much of yourself in your relationships and not feeling that this is being reciprocated. This may or may not indicate what is truly happening in your relationship, as it can also indicate that you are giving away too much of yourself as a people pleaser and have unrealistic expectations of what people are willing to give back in return, leaving you feeling emotionally bankrupt.

Naked Dreams

Dreams of being naked, especially in a classroom or public-speaking environment, are usually associated with anxiety about taking a test or being judged in a public environment of one's peers. It's pretty obvious that this dream typically means laying oneself bare, exposed, and open to others.

What I have found to be most interesting about this kind of dream is that many people who have it often describe finding that their body looks better in the dream than in real life. This is a good sign, meaning that your self-esteem is pretty good and that while you are stressing about a particular situation, like public speaking, overall you have a healthy attitude about your capabilities and what you can handle.

It's important to notice how you react in the dream when you realize that you are naked. What part of the body do you cover in the dream?

When you become a master dreamer, you'll learn how to interact in the dream while experiencing it, so you'll be able to change your posture and how you feel. For example, you may have a dream of being naked in which you are crouched down and trying to cover certain areas while feeling embarrassed. When you can become consciously aware in your dream, you may proudly walk to the front of the classroom or podium, shoulders pulled back, head held high, with a big smile on your face.

This might not feel possible right now, but in upcoming chapters I'm going to show you how this can be achieved. For now I hope it at least brings a smile to your face to imagine changing a naked dream from something uncomfortable to something bold and empowering.

Pregnancy Dreams

For women, they usually are the one pregnant in a pregnancy dream, and for men, the dream is about a woman they know becoming pregnant. Surprisingly, dreams about being pregnant are rarely about the real thing.

They more often indicate a big change and something new coming into your life.

Most typically when a dream indicates that a pregnancy is coming to you, you will dream about the baby, rather than the pregnancy, in ways such as holding a newborn baby and experiencing warm feelings of love and happiness. Pregnancy indicates something new coming your way, so in the dream, look at what stage of pregnancy you are in. Are you about to give birth, or are you newly pregnant? This will help establish a time frame of when this new change is coming in your life. If you are in labor, how intense is the labor? This will give clues to how challenging this new change will feel. Who is helping you give birth in the dream—your partner or a midwife, who might be a friend that you recognize? This can indicate who will be there to support you through this big change.

If the dream is about becoming pregnant, such as having sex with your partner and then realizing you have become pregnant. and you feel happy about this news, it indicates that you and your partner have shared goals and are growing closer together with your life plans and dreams. If you feel worried during this type of dream and are nervous that you might become pregnant, it can mean you are worried about the stability and support missing in the relationship.

Sex Dreams

Another common type of dream is a sexual dream, in which you are engaged in sexual relations of some kind. These are very complex dreams, and it is difficult to give an example of what one might mean. Many times sex dreams are really about you rather than the partner in your dream. You may be awakening to experiencing a greater depth of emotional connection and passion or feeling bolder in life.

Sex is connected to the second chakra, which is also the chakra of creativity, so a sex dream can actually represent the subconscious mind working to open the conscious mind to being creative and artistic. Many times, sex dreams are awakening pent-up desires that are not being released, which could directly be about your sex life but may also be about wishes, dreams, and goals that have gone unfulfilled for some time.

In some sex dreams, you may be surprised to find that you have switched roles. If you are a woman, you may dream that you have a penis and are taking on the role of a man. This is a sign that you are balancing your masculine and feminine sides within, which we all have, and are seeking to bring them into balance. It may indicate that your spiritual progress is going very well and that your two inner natures are working well together. It indicates strength and the ability to harness and work equally with your masculine and feminine natures.

When you have a sex dream with a stranger or someone that is not your partner, it does not always indicate that you are considering an affair. Many times, it means that you are opening up to new opportunities in life. This usually doesn't mean that you are going to have sexual relations with that person, but rather that on a subconscious level you are ready to have new adventures and experiences and try new things.

Uncomfortable sex dreams, in which the sex is against your will, for example, often indicate that you have not found your voice in life to speak about what you really want in a relationship or in life. These dreams indicate that you need to learn how to step into your personal power and take back some control.

Teeth Dreams

Another common dream is about teeth: missing teeth, having all of your teeth fall out while speaking or smiling, and, strangely, dining in public and your teeth almost always fall out into your plate at the table. Most often these dreams are connected with anxiety over a particular situation or concerns about aging and feeling less powerful.

Women tend to have this dream more often than men and it's often connected to a situation where they feel they have lost influence over people or situations. These dreams occur most often in conjunction with major life changes. Children have this dream often when they are losing their baby teeth and when they are going through puberty, and women experience this dream most often when they are going through menopause.

Water Dreams

One of the most common dream symbols found in dreams is the presence of water in one form or another. This is discussed further in the appendix, but it's important to bring it to your attention now because it is so predominant. Water most often indicates your emotional well-being in the dream.

If the water is choppy and rough and stormy, you are very upset emotionally about what's happening in the dream. If the water is calm and flowing gently, you are at peace with what's occurring in the dream. If the water is deep and still, there is still much to be revealed about the subject that you are dreaming about.

At this point, I hope it's becoming clear that while there are some generalities in understanding dreams, to really interpret dreams you have to go beyond the generic dream dictionary and delve deeper into your thoughts and feelings and what is happening in your life.

The problem with most dream dictionaries is that the meanings come from various cultures and can be associated with cultural mores of the time as well as the morals and superstitions of those people. Many of these no longer apply in today's world.

In creating your dream notebook, you are in a sense taking your notes and observations from interpreting your dreams and then writing your own dream dictionary, which will serve you much better in this work.

Creating a Dream Workbook

It's time to start converting your dream journal into a proper workbook. Now that you are able to remember your dreams and record them and are learning how to look objectively at and intuitively interpret your daily life dreams, it's time to compile the dreams into categories.

Step 1: Categorize Your Dreams

Look at your dreams and determine into which of the four main categories each should be organized. As a reminder, the four categories are:

Daily Life Dreams: Dreams about things on your mind and subconscious that you are working through in daily life. These types of dreams allow us to work through troubling events and personal experiences when we are unsure of how to handle these experiences properly on an emotional level.

Prophetic Dreams: Intuitive dreams about people, places, and events to come.

Teaching Dreams: The higher self journeys to the other side to explore and learn.

Visitation Dreams: Loved ones and guides in the spirit world visit.

Separate your dreams into these categories. It's important to note that they may fit into several categories, as prophetic dreams often include visitation dreams as well, and so on.

Step 2: Create Subcategories

Subcategorize the dreams into groups that you can easily reference in the future. The categories should include groups such as dreams about family members, dreams about your life, dreams about the area of the world where you live, dreams in which you visit with family and friends who have passed on, dreams in which you connect with spirit guides, and dreams that are so mysterious that you are not sure what they mean.

Step 3: Take Note of the Symbols

Once the dreams have been separated into these sections, make notes about all the symbols that you have noticed in the dreams as well as how often these same symbols appear.

Symbols can include a variety of things, such as a family pet that always appears with you in a dream; a guide, seen or unseen, who appears to accompany you in dreams; and random items that appear frequently in dreams, such as a type of tree, a bicycle, car, other types of vehicles, wild and domestic animals, flowers, gemstones, a bag of money, or items that are specifically meaningful to you (a house you grew up in, for example).

In essence, what you are doing here is becoming a dream detective/analyst. You are becoming the expert on your dreams, and there is no expert better than you in interpreting your own. This is because the symbols and items in your dreams are more meaningful to you, and it is easier for you to directly correlate why certain items appear in your dreams. Perhaps you've noticed that I often say what a symbol *can* mean, rather than what it *will* mean. This is because dreams are incredibly subjective and unique. There are common dream symbols, but even these can change meaning according to what is happening in the dream. There is no one-size-fits-all dream, nor can any book specifically describe what each dream means.

Now you've learned how to take your dream journal and turn it into a dream workbook so that you can analyze and interpret what your dreams are trying to tell you. Take this time to go back over the dream journal you've been keeping and convert your notes into a workbook that is better organized. Many people create a dream database on the computer that makes it easier to search for specific details. As your dream workbook grows, you may find it to be a helpful tool, as over time you'll be recording hundreds of dreams.

By this time, you've been regularly recording your dreams, you've been setting goals and intentions to remember your dreams, and perhaps you've been asking your higher self to help you remember your dreams in greater detail. At this point, you are well on your way to interpreting your dreams.

Three

PROPHETIC AND RECURRING DREAMS

Prophetic dreams are dreams that show evidence of precognition. "Precognition" means knowledge of something in the future before it occurs. It's the ability to see future events—in short, what psychics do, using their honed skills of ESP and at times engaging in the use of tools such as tarot cards, runes, astrology, crystal gazing, and others, like their dreams.

Perhaps the most famous person who had the ability to be prophetic in a dream state was Edgar Cayce, who is known as the "sleeping prophet." For over forty years, Cayce gave thousands of psychic readings by lying down with his eyes closed and going into a meditative state that connected him with his superconscious state of being. He never had any intention of being a psychic originally, though he was a deeply spiritual man.

Over fourteen thousand of Edgar Cayce's readings were recorded, and they can be read today in the library at the Edgar Cayce Association for Research and Enlightenment in Virginia. His dream-state predictions cover thousands of topics, with a great majority of them helping people treat their illnesses and medical conditions. Other topics he covered in his dream state include reincarnation, dream interpretations, ancient mysteries (including information about the pyramids in Egypt), and amazing psychic and spiritual phenomena.

Cayce was a master of using the superconscious dream state in order to see the past and the future and to tap into the global consciousness and into the higher spiritual planes to obtain information from current and previous lifetimes as well as history of humanity since its beginning.

A person with precognitive or psychic ability can tune into this information when they are awake. Prophetic dreams, on the other hand, happen while sleeping, and the person may not have any idea or indication that they have any intuitive ability at all. In fact, they may vehemently deny that they have intuitive ability and may have opposing spiritual beliefs that disagree with the thought of possessing psychic ability or prophecy. There are records of prophetic dreams in all cultures throughout history as well as written records of prophecy in the Bible. Many people, though, are uncomfortable with the thought that they could have a prophetic dream.

When a person has a prophetic dream, it can be very disturbing to them, especially if they don't believe in the ability to see the future. They wake up with their heart pounding from a terrifying dream warning them of danger to come, or they experience a physical pain in the body warning them of a problem. The dream itself is a terrifying experience, only exacerbated further when the event happens in real life.

The most frustrating part of having prophetic dreams is that you typically have no idea when they will occur and can't seem to order them at will when you desire to know something. There isn't much you can do to force yourself to have prophetic dreams. They most often come when least expected and often with information that you knew nothing about previously. I write about them here more to explain how they feel and how you can determine if they are prophetic if they do happen to you one day.

Sometimes prophetic dreams come in enough time to give fair warning, to help change someone's destiny. There are stories of kings, queens, emperors, and others who were spared from death through prophetic dreams that they or their spiritual advisors had. They paid attention to these dreams and changed their plan of action, which saved them.

In other situations, a person can have a prophetic dream, but it lacks the detailed information needed in order to save them from the experience. Abraham Lincoln is a famous example of someone who experienced a prophetic dream: he attended his own funeral. He was being shown that his death was near, but the dream did not give him details of how and when it would occur, so there was little he could do to change or delay the future outcome.

Some of the most traumatic prophetic dreams that I've had are ones that involved me personally. These dreams were so haunting that I remember them as clearly today as I did when they occurred many years ago.

Those of you reading this who have experienced a similar type of dream know what I speak of. You wake from the dream with every fiber of your being on alert, knowing that something terrible is going to occur and, try what you will, you can't shake the dream and go back to sleep, nor can you shake it off throughout the day.

In the introduction of this book, I shared with you my prophetic dream about losing my dog. When your dreams are this intense, they most typically are warning you of something to come. I learned two valuable lessons from these early dreams: one, I could not always control what happened to the people and pets that I cared for in my life; and two, I was being prepared for a lifetime as a psychic and empath, in which many times I could see and sometimes feel the future.

I've continued to have many prophetic dreams throughout my lifetime, and not all of them have been this traumatic or life altering. Many of the dreams have warned me of problems to come, including conflicts that I could not stop. These dreams helped me be better prepared for the conflicts when they arrived, including being more emotionally ready for the argument or negative experience another person would bring into my life. I've also had prophetic dreams in which I was given enough time to warn the person about what was to come in order to help them avoid a dangerous experience.

Over time, my assumption has been that when I have a prophetic dream in which there is nothing I can do to change the situation, this is divine will. In these cases, I am receiving the message, picking up the waves in motion like a radio. Perhaps this was the case for Abraham Lincoln as well.

In other cases, I dream about something happening to someone, and I have time to tell them and give them the opportunity to do something about it. I assume that I have been given this prophetic dream in order to help this person, as it is not necessarily their time to have this experience.

The challenging thing about prophetic dreams is that if you have one and warn the person and they avoid the experience, many times you both will never know if it would have occurred. Given the opportunity, though, I'm always happy to warn the person so that they can make a change and avoid the experience, even if they don't believe it would have happened.

I've now had enough prophetic dreams that people listen to me and heed the warnings. Some of these dreams include warning people in New Orleans and Mississippi about Hurricane Katrina. When I was younger, I didn't really share with people that I was psychic and had prophetic dreams, so it was much more difficult to share these types of dreams with others.

I once had a dream about a friend's mother. I woke up in a panic from this dream, calling my friend early in the morning to tell her that I had a dream about her mother and that she should not drive to work because she would be in a car accident where she would be injured. The friend didn't believe me about the dream and didn't warn her mother. Later that morning when the car accident with her mother occurred as I described, she was understandably very upset. She called me to tell me it had happened as I had explained. I thought at first that she was calling to say that she wished she would have warned her mother to stay home that morning. To my surprise, she called to yell at me and say that whatever this ability was that I had, it had caused this problem. I remember being so shocked and hurt by this accusation, as I had been trying to help. I can't blame her for being upset because I had never shared with her that I had dreams like these, so it was a shock to her system in many ways.

In another scenario, I warned a friend that her family was in danger of having their home flooded from a storm coming to the state where they lived. She disregarded this information, thinking there was no way that I could predict these kinds of events. When the storm came and her family was flooded out of their home, she called me later to discuss what I had told her. She said that she understood it to be true that I must have some kind of ability but that it was one that she did not agree with and that she thought was a bad thing spiritually. Rather than appreciating that she could have moved her family out of the town before the storm flooded their home and area, she asked that I never share this type of information with her again, as she did not want to know anything about it due to her religious beliefs. I've respected her wishes and have not spoken about these types of things with her again.

I mention these instances to prepare you for when you have prophetic dreams. They may not always be received in the helpful manner you intend. In both of these situations, it was the early days when I had not begun to talk so openly about my psychic abilities to many people. It was a surprise to both of these friends when I warned them after a prophetic dream. Now that I've written many books and taught thousands of people about these abilities, people take it and me more seriously.

Had my friend warned her mother about the car accident and her mother stayed home, the accident would not have occurred, and so there would have been no proof if my dream was prophetic or not. That's the challenge with prophetic dreams: with many of them, if you heed them, you aren't sure if the event would have happened.

Some can be tracked; for example, you dream of a plane crash and warn someone not to get on a certain flight, and then that tragedy does indeed happen. My friend and her mother could have checked traffic reports that morning to see if an accident had occurred on the roads that she traveled to work during her commute time, and that might have provided the proof they needed. However, even this is hard to say, because some experiences happen at certain times and need certain people in play for them to happen, so there may have not been an accident that morning because the mother was not there.

This is what is so frustrating about prophetic experiences. There are so many variables that are not fully understood, so they are difficult to track scientifically and typically are not repeatable. Throw in the fact that the variables change through energy of what we think, feel, and do, thus changing the outcome, and we are dealing with quantum physics well beyond what science understands yet at this level.

If you have prophetic dreams, it's important to be as gentle as possible when explaining your dream to the person you had the dream about.

In the case of my friend's mother, I called urgently, as I had woken from the dream only minutes before my friend's mother was about to leave for work, so I didn't have the time to get into a deep explanation—I was trying to stop her from getting into her car. My friend was very upset and shaken from what happened to her mother, and I felt so bad that I had not shared with her earlier that I had psychic abilities, which occasionally showed up in dreams. Had she known this about me earlier, she would have taken the news much better.

In the second example about the coming storm, my friend had heard me speak about psychic ability and that I could see and predict things, but she never took it seriously and didn't like discussing the topic with me, so our friendship focused on other things. When I made the call to tell her about the flood near her family, the reality of me being able to see a situation like this was more than she could comfortably bear with her personal religious beliefs. She disengaged with the friendship after this event, as she felt uncomfortable around me going forward.

I'm fortunate to have other friends who are fine with and very understanding of my peculiar abilities. You may find for yourself that as you open up to understanding your dreams, you may experience prophetic dreams as well.

If at all possible, take the time first to explain to the person that you have had a dream that appears to be a warning. State that there is no way that you can be absolutely sure that this dream will come true, but that you felt so strongly about the dream that you wanted to share it with them in case it could be of help. Be careful when doing this, however. If you have never had a prophetic dream, you could scare someone unnecessarily with information that is not really a prediction of things to come.

Positive Prophetic Dreams

I hope I haven't scared you off too badly about prophetic dreams. My intent is to warn you about how they can be disturbing to both you and others so that you are prepared should you have one. Many of my clients, students, and friends have shared stories with me that they or someone in their family have experienced a prophetic dream in their life at one time or another, so chances are pretty good that you may have had one or will one day.

Not all prophetic dreams are so foreboding. There are times when you'll have wonderful prophetic dreams about the future. As we discussed in an earlier chapter, many people have dreamt about their future child and seen a first glimpse of their baby in the dreams before they even become pregnant. I've had happy dreams in which I've seen homes that I will live in and even new relationships to come.

One particular prophetic dream recurred often throughout my life. In the dream, which I first had at the age of sixteen, I was married in a past lifetime around two thousand years ago. I remembered distinct details in this dream and wrote them down in my dream journal. The man was kind and loving, and his name was James. We had a wonderful marriage and life together and pursued our spiritual work as part of our daily lives. Each time at the end of the dream, the man I was married to would say to me, "When we meet again in another lifetime, you'll recognize me as James. I will find a way to show you that I am James."

I became convinced over time that the man I would meet and marry would find a way to show me he was James. Either James would literally be his first, middle, or last name, or he would remember this lifetime and describe it to me. When I married for the first time when I was very young, I remember looking hard at the person to see if he was James, but he was not. I decided that perhaps it was just a dream and that we would not be able to connect again in this lifetime. This relationship ended fairly quickly in a divorce and was not meant to be.

Years later when I wasn't looking to even date anyone, I had a friend who decided to introduce me to someone that she thought would be a good match for me. I declined the offer and thanked her for thinking of me. She was persistent, however, and invited me to a birthday party that she was throwing for someone I knew. I came to the party and discovered that she had invited him as well. She made it very obvious when she introduced us that she had intended for us to meet.

As soon as we met, we both felt a spark and an instant connection. He told me his first name, which was not James, but I could not deny that I felt like I had known this man for a lifetime. We had a long talk that evening about spiritual topics and went on our first date a few days later. On the second date, I asked questions like I often do, such as what his birthdate was, because I wanted to know his astrology sign and information. I also asked him what his full name was, and his middle name was James. This excited and intrigued me, but wasn't enough to fully go on for me.

A couple of weeks later, he called me on the phone and proceeded to tell me that he had a dream about me the night before and that it was a different type of dream because he saw himself in a past life. He relayed that I was with him in that dream as his partner. I couldn't believe it—he was describing the recurring dream that I had experienced over the years.

I stopped him at that moment and said, "Don't tell me anything else about this dream. Stop right now and write down everything you remember about this dream."

He replied, "I already have. I write down all of my dreams."

Hello, I remember thinking, *is this my dream guy literally or what? He's into all of the metaphysical things that I'm into and he even journals his dreams.*

I said, "I'm coming over to discuss your dream."

"Great!" he said.

I went digging into a big box where I kept my journals and grabbed two of them in which I had recorded this recurring dream over the years with different details. When I arrived at his place, I handed him my dream journals and asked if I could see his. We exchanged journals and began to read. At several points of reading each other's descriptions about this past-life dream, we would both be a little surprised and shocked, glance up at each other, and then continue reading.

When we were done, we couldn't believe it. We had both had the same dream, the same remembering of a lifetime together, that we had both detailed and explained with the same memories and experiences. The details were so similar it was uncanny. His details focused a little more on the man's perspective of what life was like at that time, and mine had the more feminine observations, but it was the same life and the same dream. What each of us had felt the most in that dream was the strong, loving relationship that we had shared. He remembered that his name was James in the dream, and when he read my dream about how he said he would find me again and would find a way to show me he was James, it was just overwhelming.

From this moment onward, we began our adventures together in this lifetime as we explored other prophetic dreams we had over the years along with remembrances of many previous lifetimes and experiences together, including times we had studied together in ancient Egypt and Greece in the mystery schools and other times when the studies were more informal with teachers and guides.

The more we worked together, the more powerful our experiences grew, and our psychic connection was linked. We once studied with a metaphysical teacher and over time began to feel that this particular teacher was not leading us in a good direction. We decided to link our energy together one evening as we lay together in bed and ask that we be given clear information about this person through our dreams in order to determine if we should continue to study with them.

When we awoke the next morning, we both immediately wrote down our dreams before speaking to each other. Our dreams again were eerily similar. Both of us had dreamed of a past lifetime when we were students together, and this person had been our teacher. In the dream, the teacher had turned to the dark side and was using their energy to take energy from others. The teacher was here again in this lifetime attempting to do the same thing. We knew that our intuition and feelings were right on target and that we shouldn't continue studying or engaging with this person.

I could list hundreds of dreams like these in which I've been able to divine prophetic information about past lives as well as what's happening in my current life. In some cases, I've also been able to dream about what's coming, beyond this current lifetime and into a future lifetime.

Over time as you continue your work with dreams, you'll find that you'll be able to explore the past, present, and future in ways you never imagined before.

Prophetic Dreams Workbook

As you are keeping your dream workbook, make sure to dedicate a special section to prophetic dreams.

Date each dream and write down as much descriptive information that you can, including how emotionally intense you felt about the dream. The details and symbols in these dreams are very important and can help discern what the dream really means and how literal it is.

Some prophetic dreams can be more symbolic than specific. For example, you may dream about a death that is not actually a death, but rather an ending of something, like a relationship that ends in divorce or a friendship that is going to come to a sudden and rocky ending.

This is why the dream workbook is so important, as over time you'll have a much better understanding about your dreams and how you feel about each one. You'll be better able to determine if the dreams are warning you about a specific situation or hinting to you about an emotional experience that is heading your direction.

In daily life, we tend to remember the negative experiences more strongly than the positive ones. We can receive ten compliments in one day, but if one person says something negative about us, that is what we will focus on for days or even longer. This is part of human nature, and it runs the same with dreams.

For example, in the dream that my husband and I shared about when he was James, parts of the dream focused on different details that were important to us individually. Our dreams both described our home and the town where we lived in great detail. However, what was most important to us in daily life was a little different. As the wife, I remembered how my home looked and felt, while he remembered more about his work life. Some of the parts that matched the closest in our dreams were things that happened that were surprising and negative, such as when something caught fire in the home and an upsetting incident with livestock.

When we have a very upsetting dream, we tend to remember it in great detail in comparison to the happy prophetic dreams, which don't feel as real to us in the dream or in life. When many people are asked to describe their happy prophetic dream, a smile will cross their face and they talk about the dream like it is a vague idea that they wish could come true but probably won't. Yet when asked to describe a scary prophetic dream, they seem almost certain that it's destined to happen.

It's difficult to give specific steps on how to have a prophetic dream because 99 percent of the time they come out of the blue with no warning at all. You can try asking your guides to help you dream about something that will happen in the future, but this is so nebulous that it usually works better to ask for help in finding the solution to a current problem. Prophetic dreams are the most mysterious of all and for the most part cannot be tamed, controlled, or timed.

Recurring Dreams

A recurring dreams is a dream that appears repeatedly. You recognize it from previous dreams because it is so strange to have this dream over and over again. If you're keeping a dream journal, you'll find that how the dream ends rarely changes. It's like watching a movie that you've already seen and playing it over again. The more you have a recurring dream, though, the more details you'll notice and be able to record.

Some of the most common recurring dreams are dreams that I've mentioned earlier, including dreams of falling, flying, and being chased. When these types of dreams recur, they are typically the subconscious mind trying to help you work through something you are facing in your daily life. These dreams can be very helpful, as they motivate you to take action on something that is disturbing you or making you uncomfortable. For example, a dream about being naked in a classroom before you take a test can cause you to double down on studying in order to make sure that you are as prepared as you can possibly be to take the test. Recurring dreams feel stressful when you experience them, but in reality your subconscious is trying to help your sense of confidence and well-being. These types of dreams fall under the daily life category of dreams.

Recurring dreams can be a result of post-traumatic stress disorder (PTSD). People who have suffered trauma may repeatedly dream about the incident over and over. Their subconscious mind is trying to help them come to terms with what occurred so that they can process the grief, pain, and fear through the dream state, as many times it is too difficult for the conscious mind to deal with for a long period of time. These dreams fall into the category of what we also describe as nightmares.

A rarer form of a recurring dream that goes beyond the description of nightmare is the night terror. The biggest difference between a nightmare and a night terror is that a nightmare occurs during the REM state of sleep, in which most dreams occur, while the night terror occurs during a non-REM state. In this case, the person many times does not remember the dream. They may sit up in bed and scream out loud, only to fall right back asleep. When awakened, they often don't recall the dream or screaming, and they are surprised to hear that this occurred when another person describes it to them. Many people have described an episode of this type with a child or a partner who was talking out loud, screaming, or thrashing around in the bed. Night terrors are pretty rare to experience.

Another type of sleep disorder of this nature is sleep walking, which is experienced more often by children for a brief period of time. Adults who sleep walk are usually under the influence of a medication that they have taken to sleep, only to experience the side effect of sleep walking. In chapter 7, we'll further explore nightmares in general.

The REM stage of sleep typically occurs every hour and a half to two hours of sleep throughout the night. Thus, the longer you sleep, the more dreams you can have each evening. The REM stage for each person can differ from ten minutes to thirty minutes or more. Your dreams and dream cycles are unique to you and your sleep patterns. Additionally, your dream cycles and sleeping patterns will change throughout your life, sometimes due to stress and life changes as well as evolving as we age.

The studies of dreams still show that we don't know much about dreams, including why they occur or why some people dream in greater detail than others.

Prophetic Recurring Dreams

When the recurring dream is about something less ordinary and becomes more specific about an event that you don't recognize as happening in your life, then the likelihood exists that it is a prophetic dream that is repeating and trying to warn you of something to come.

There are many reports about people who have recurring dreams that warn of an event to come as well as reports of large groups of people who share a recurring prophetic dream. Shamans were more familiar with this and often relied on this information to warn them of things to come to assist with their survival, including dreams about major weather changes like floods and famine, so they could prepare in advance and store food or migrate elsewhere when necessary. They would also dream about coming wars and battles to give them time to prepare.

One very famous case of a disastrous prophetic dream involved a group of children in Wales who didn't want to go to school because of their dreams. These schoolchildren woke panicked from recurring nightmares in which they were in darkness and feeling crushed and unable to breathe. The children's dreams were eerily similar. Some of the dreams were documented, as several adults had the same dream, including a local housewife and other people of Welsh descent who were living in other areas of the United Kingdom.

This prophetic recurring dream happened several days before the incident in 1966, when a coal slide disaster buried and destroyed a portion of town, including a local school, where 116 children between the ages of seven and ten lost their lives as they were crushed under the weight of the coal that poured over their school, making it the worst landslide disaster in the United Kingdom. Some of these children had reported their dreams of being buried alive in the school several days before the event occurred. One child reportedly had awoken from her dream two days prior to tell her mother that she was not afraid of dying because she would be with her two friends when it occurred.

Other examples of disastrous recurring prophetic dreams by large groups of people about natural and manmade disasters are September 11 in New York City, the death of Princess Diana, and Hurricane Katrina in New Orleans. Many people have shared their dreams leading up to these events while not fully understanding the dreams or what they were trying to communicate to them.

It appears that in the global consciousness, where we have access to all the thoughts and ideas of humanity, time does not exist in the same way that it does here on the earth plane. When an incident of great tragedy is drawing near, it seems that it can be detected days or sometimes weeks before it occurs and that some people can pick up on this emotional energy through their dreams because the grief and pain is so intense and on a large scale.

The majority of recurring dreams, though, are the daily life type of dreams. Prophetic dreams don't recur as often. They typically get their point across in a very powerful and profound way, and you wake up feeling as if you've lived through the experience on a very direct and intense level. There are some prophetic dreams that don't repeat the exact recurring dream; rather, the dream shifts each time about the same recurring subject. I refer to these dreams as status updates, providing information about what will occur and how it's currently changing.

This has been a very serious discussion about prophetic and recurring dreams. I wish it could be more lighthearted, but for some reason many prophetic dreams that people remember do seem to concentrate on very terrible and disastrous events. Perhaps it is because the emotions felt with the pain are so much more intense that more people pick up on this energy over happier experiences.

This seems to be the case in the beginning for many people as they remember their dreams. But if you do the work that I've described so far in this book and continue to work on remembering your dreams, you'll be much more open to remembering other prophetic dreams, including dreams of past lives with hints of how they will reappear again in this lifetime.

In future chapters, we'll explore how you can change your thinking and your attitude about dreams and how you can empower yourself to believe in the power of your good dreams.

Four

TEACHING DREAMS

Teaching dreams occur when the superconscious, or higher self, journeys to the other side to explore and learn. I also affectionately describe this to my students as "going to night school."

The more you work on remembering your dreams, the more you are engaging in connecting your subconscious mind with your conscious mind, and with a bit more effort, you can connect both of these minds to the superconscious mind.

The superconscious mind, which I describe as the part of you that is connected directly to your soul, is the higher spiritual aspect of yourself that has access to the global consciousness. The global consciousness is an energy field where all the thoughts and ideas from humanity are stored. This field also has direct access to the higher energetic planes, often described as the spiritual planes, where access to thoughts and ideas and inspiration from spirit guides and other spiritual beings can be found. The ancient Greeks described access to these planes as being able to speak to the Muses or to the gods.

Once you've begun to train your mind to remember your dreams, you can become more consciously aware in your dreams. As you'll find in chapter 6, you can also learn to lucid dream, through which you'll interact with a dream and change it at will.

For now, though, the next step is to awaken the conscious mind so that you can program it to stay alert during your dreamtime and to open both it and the subconscious mind to connect to the superconscious mind while dreaming.

This is an incredibly helpful technique to have—you can work through a problem by essentially sleeping on it!

Exercise: Higher Learning through Your Dreams

In this exercise, you will be programming your mind to connect to your higher self. This allows the superconscious part of yourself, which exists beyond the confines of the human body and beyond space and time on earth, to search the global consciousness to find a solution to your problem.

As you work on this technique, you will receive brief answers in reply to your problem. The exciting thing is if you continue to work on these techniques, your superconscious will awaken and want to reach out more often to the global conscious field and the energy fields in the higher planes in order to learn more and evolve.

This begins what I described as night school. Your dreams move from just being requests to answer a problem in your life to receiving downloads of information through your dream state that enhance your personal journey here in this lifetime.

Step 1: Create Sacred Space

To begin activating your mind to be receptive to this type of information in a dream state, I suggest to my students that they first engage in this exercise while they are awake.

The most effective way to focus your mind to get into this groove is through a guided meditation. The type of meditation that you want to participate in for this type of work is one that allows you to meet and work with your spirit guide. A guide is often helpful to people when first starting this work, as it can feel like too big of a leap or journey to believe that you can access this information by yourself as a beginner. Bringing in a guide establishes a comfort level and baseline to begin this journey.

Here's an example of one type of scene that I create in a guided meditation, which creates a sacred space:

To begin, picture a beautiful garden area with a thick, lush, vibrant green lawn. As you step onto the grass, feel your feet sink deep into the plush carpet of these green leaves. A soft scent greets you at each step, and you notice that small flowers are growing in parts of the grassy area.

Standing in the grass, feel your feet firmly connected to the ground. Raise your arms above your head, stretched outward to greet the sunlight in order to pull the pure white light from the rays of the sun around you and into your body.

Visualize this pure white light covering your body and say,

> *I am surrounded by the pure white light.*
> *Only that which is for my highest and best*
> *may be made manifest through to me.*
> *I ask for divine guidance and divine wisdom.*
> *Thank you.*

You don't have to say this particular prayer, but it is wise to say a protective prayer or mantra of some kind so that as you open up to the other side, you are surrounded by only the highest and best forces of good who can send information to you in this regard.

At this point, you have surrounded your body and the energy field around you known as the aura in this pure white light. This spiritually protects you during your meditation, and you are now open to engaging with the higher self and other beings from the spiritual planes. The act of sinking your feet into the beautiful deep, soft green grass has grounded you to the earth plane while allowing your mind to prepare to travel to the other realms.

Now return your focus to where you are standing in the grassy area and notice that there is a path before you made of smooth stones that create an easy walkway. You are barefoot, and the stones feel warm and comforting as they support you on this journey.

As you walk ahead, the path leads you into a secret garden, covered with flowers, on the left side of the path. On the right is a very big tree. In front of you on the path is a river that is gently moving, and to the left is a waterfall streaming over a group of rocks. The river continues to the right side as far as you can see. There in front of the river is a bench where you can comfortably sit and enjoy the river.

As you sit on the bench, take notice of your surroundings. What kinds of flowers are growing in the garden? Is the garden just beginning to bloom, or is it in full bloom? What colors are the flowers? What kind of tree is on your right—is it in full bloom with green leaves, in the colors of fall, or bare, without leaves? How big is the trunk and how far do the branches spread?

Before you is the river. How does the river look to you? Do you see fish moving about? How about the waterfall—what speed is the water moving, how fast is the current, and how tall is the waterfall?

In this step, you are taking notice of what your surroundings are expressing to you in this subconscious manner. This practice is similar to interpreting what your surroundings are expressing to you in your dreams.

Step 2: Meet Your Spirit Guide

Sit and take in all of these scenes until you are comfortable with this space and can describe it in great detail. Then when you are ready, ask for your spirit guide to enter this sacred space and to come sit on the bench next to you. Spirit guides are helpers from the other side who were assigned to be with us before our birth. They assist us throughout each lifetime with our destined purpose and soul journey.

Visualize your spirit guide. Are they male or female? Are they someone you know, or is this the first time you've seen them? Are they dressed in clothing that is contemporary or from another time period? What light do you see around them, or what type of energy do you feel while in their presence?

Welcome them to your sacred space and invite them to sit with you and take in the beauty of what you have created here in the garden and in the water.

When you are ready, begin a conversation with them and explain that you would like to visit with them here from time to time in this sacred space in order to ask questions and to receive their help with problems and concerns you are facing in this lifetime.

See tip 6 for alternatives to talking with a spirit guide.

Step 3: Communicate with Your Spirit Guide

Now deep in this meditation, ask your spirit guide the first question that you have on your mind.

Be prepared that the message may come to you in a variety of ways. The guide may turn to you and answer you directly, or they may show you an answer through an image that appears in your sacred space.

For example, a deer may enter in front of you and nibble in the garden, a butterfly may flitter by, or a fish may jump out of the river. The weather may suddenly change here in this space: the sunlight may grow very bright or clouds may darken the skies as the wind picks up around you. An unexpected image may also occur, such as a rose suddenly blooming in the garden or a gemstone appearing at your feet.

When you first begin this exercise, if you are not well practiced at meditation, it may feel forced and will take you some time to do this type of creative visualization. Continue to practice creating this sacred space in your meditation, working at it at least once a week or, if you have the time, every other day, until you can visualize this scene so well that you find that after a few weeks' time you can prepare to meditate, visualize your space, and instantly find yourself there in the garden.

You may not yet be receiving answers from your guide when you ask them, but this is still very important work, as you are forming an energetic conscious grid that is creating a space for communication to come through from the superconscious mind.

Step 4: Bringing Sacred Space into Dreamtime

Once your visualization has been established at this level while awake, it's time to take it to the next level. In the evening as you prepare to go to sleep, follow the process you have created with this meditation and visualize your sacred space.

Now as you are in this space, ask your question that you are seeking an answer to and instead of waiting for the answer in the moment, allow yourself to drift off to sleep. Ask that the answer be provided to you in your dream state and that upon awakening you will remember the answer you received.

This is a highly effective technique, as you are letting go of the conscious mind, which tries to control the outcome or second-guess the answer you are seeking. In the active meditation when awake, it's more difficult to stop the conscious mind from taking over and trying to mold and control what happens when you ask the question.

In the dream state, the conscious mind is quieted and the superconscious mind can take over and reach far beyond your inner thoughts in order to provide inspiration and new ideas to help with the answer you seek. When you awake, immediately jot down your dream and any details that feel important. It's important to note that speaking to your superconscious and to your spirit guides does not mean that all of the answers to life will be provided to you.

Generally, the information you receive will offer an inspired idea of what to do next, without solving the entire problem at hand. This is why they are called teaching dreams, as they are helping and instructing you on how to evolve without spoon-feeding you all the answers. This is how the system universally seems to be set up, which is part of the journey of our spiritual and our human experience.

What is most comforting in this practice is that you are now able to access a much larger energy plane of inspired ideas and information. You have learned how to access this information all through your dreams.

Helpful Tips for This Teaching Dream Exercise

Tip 1: The definition of sacred space is open to your interpretation.

The meditation in the garden described in step 1 to create sacred space is just an example of one type of environment. Create any type of environment like this that feels right and comfortable to you.

I've had students create classroom environments for their meditation in which different guides appeared similar to professors they had in college. Others created a sailboat and sailed from port to port in their sacred space meditation to meet with different teachers and guides.

The possibilities are endless and only limited by your imagination. The sacred space that my husband visualized was a large room filled with computers. In his meditative and dream state, he would sit at the console keyboard and type in his question and receive the answer on the computer screen.

The sacred space should be as unique as the individual, as the goal is to create a comfortable environment where you can open your mind to this level of interaction.

Some people prefer a more controlled environment, like my late husband did with his room full of computers. In his sacred space, the information only came to him when he typed a question into the computer. It was a very controlled environment where he was mostly in charge of what would occur in this situation.

On the flip side, I'm comfortable with the idea of being in the garden where anything can and will change in the moment. I like the idea of new experiences occurring beyond my control or imagination.

As I'm chatting with my guides, animals come and go, the weather changes, the pace of the river ebbs and flows, flowers bloom and wither in the garden, and even the tree shakes and the branches sway when the winds pick up as I ask a very emotional question. This works for my personality, as I'm very connected to my emotional state.

If you prefer a more controlled and peaceful environment, create a space that offers less opportunity for things to change around you. Some people ask to receive the information written on a piece of paper inside an envelope that is handed to them to read alone. Others create a small room where they enter through a door to ask their question and receive an answer. Then as they walk back through the door out of the room, everything dissolves and goes away.

The more you engage in this practice, the deeper you can go, and the more comfortable you are with this practice, the stranger it may become, as different guides and beings will appear as well as various animals and symbols to show you things.

You are in control of how much you want to see and who you want to see it from, so if you feel uncomfortable with anything that appears, simply ask it to go away and ask for the information to be presented to you in a manner that is more comfortable for you.

Tip 2: Teaching dreams are so important.

These types of dream practices have been around since the dawn of mankind. Indigenous cultures have created them in sweat lodges and vision quests, helping put the mind in an altered state so that the answers sought could come from the spirit realms.

If you've read my book *The Awakened Psychic*, you'll realize that what you are engaging in is a form of telepathy between your higher self/superconscious mind and your guides. It's just one of the ways that we are all psychic and haven't been taught these tools in order to work with these natural abilities.

When you are connecting with your higher self, you are astral traveling. We all astral travel when we sleep, and you are just now more engaged in the process. With this practice, you can engage in your own vision quest using the power of your dreams.

Tip 3: If it's not working yet, remember to train your mind.

So you have the technique to receive the answers or help you seek in your dreams, but what if you are still struggling with remembering your dreams?

Nothing is more frustrating than doing all this work, creating your sacred space, visualizing it till you get it just right, and going off to sleep to get the answer, only to awake and find you can't remember.

First, it's important to remember that it's a process and to give yourself some time to train your mind to remember your dreams. Don't give up. Over time you will create a practice that works for you.

In the meantime, though, when you set up your sacred space before going to sleep and ask to remember the dream in the morning, also ask that if for any reason you don't remember the dream when you awake, your guide will send signs to you throughout the day to help with the answer to your question.

On that day, pay attention to any signs that come your way out of the blue, through people, places, and events that catch your attention. In this practice, you are programming your superconscious mind to send the information to you in this format while you are awake so that you can receive the answers you are looking for.

Tip 4: If the answers in your dreams don't make sense, ask more detailed questions.

If you find that you are receiving answers in your dream but they are so vague and nebulous that they are not helping you, there are two things you can do to fine-tune this process.

The first is to look at the question you are asking your guides and higher self. The best questions to ask are very specific and to the point.

For example, a good line of questioning regarding career would be this: "I have been offered a job at XYZ company. Should I leave my current job and take this job offer? Will this new job bring me more money and opportunity for advancement?"

This line of questioning allows for a specific answer. You may see in the dream a vision of you walking into a new office building that represents the company, and you feel happy and excited when you are inside the building. You may see a large paycheck on your desk, or you may see yourself in a conference room giving a presentation that people are appreciating. These are signs that the new job will bring the opportunity you seek.

On the other hand, you may see a vision of you leaving your old job and people shaking their heads in dismay, and then you walk outside of the building and see a gray and cloudy sky, looking like it's about to storm. This can indicate that it's not the right time to leave your current job. It depends, though, on how you ask the question and also if you have any fears regarding leaving your old job.

Alternatively, you might ask, "How is my company doing financially? Are there layoffs ahead, or should I stay at my current job?" The signs in the dream from the previous paragraph could indicate that layoffs are coming to the company, so in this case it's a good time to leave before this occurs.

It's important to be very detailed in the questions you ask and to be very specific in the way you ask them so that the answer can be as clear as possible to you in the dream state. Questions like "What's the meaning of life?" or "What should I do with my life?" or "Will I ever find a partner to love?" are too vague. The answer to what you should do with your life may not focus on what you need to do for a living in order to provide for your well-being, and the meaning of life is different for each person and can differ from lifetime to lifetime.

The same goes for asking about a partner to love. Friends can be partners in life, helping you through your journey, along with family members and sometimes even coworkers. If you are asking about a partner in a romantic setting, be specific. If you have someone in mind, ask very detailed questions about them and your relationship. If you are not seeing anyone at the moment, ask for a concept of time for when you might meet this potential life or marriage partner.

The better you become at focusing your questions, the easier the answers will come.

If you find it difficult to get just the right question, try writing it out first. Get a piece of paper and write down all the questions you have about the matter at hand. Then condense this down into what is at the heart of the question. Ask yourself, what do you truly want most to know about this situation?

Continue to cut through excess information until you have one very succinct question to ask. You may wish to write this question out on a new piece of paper and read it at your bedside before you go to sleep so that you are focused on getting the answer to that direct question. You can also take the piece of paper and slip it into your pillowcase so that you are truly "sleeping on it."

The second thing to note when looking for answers is to understand that not all answers are revealed to you, even when you ask. Some life events are part of your journey and destiny in this lifetime, and it is not meant for you to know at this time how they will unfold. If you are receiving vague answers about a question, try asking it a different way. If this does not work, ask a direct question to your guide to provide information to you that explains why the answer cannot be revealed at this time. Also ask your guide to provide any helpful hints on what you can do in the meantime.

Tip 5: Ask your spirit guides for advice.

One of the main reasons it's so important to create sacred space and then actively ask for help from your spirit guides with your question is that they can't just randomly offer you advice or answers. They have to be asked in order to engage with you and offer information. A beautiful side effect of this experience is that in their presence you will feel love, peace, and hope. Their presence alone is very comforting and reassuring.

At the same time, they are not allowed to give you the answers to every question you ask, so it can be a process to see what you can and can't discover. You have a group of spirit guides assigned to help you, so you may meet several of them over the course of doing this work.

Some guides are with you to help with your personal growth while others are assigned guides who help with specific details of your life. Many health-care workers, for example, have spirit guides who are healers and work directly with the person to help enhance their healing abilities in the medical field. When they engage in this practice, they may ask for answers in their research or on how to solve a medical problem they are working on with a patient, and that guide will be the one to answer and work with them on a breakthrough. Later, the person may ask a personal question about a relationship or buying a new home. The guide who appears would most likely be a different guide who helps in personal matters rather than medical procedures.

Tip 6: Consult other spiritual sources.

If you're not comfortable working with your spirit guides or other spiritual beings, you can ask that a family member who has crossed over to the other side be your guide. Maybe your grandfather or favorite aunt always gave you great advice and was there for you when you needed it. Now that they are in the spirit world, you can ask them to visit you in your dreams and offer their sage advice, in almost the same way as when you would visit with them here on earth.

Some people prefer to use animal totems, connecting in the dream state with an animal that they feel is their totem animal, here to teach them.

The process is uniquely independent and should be tailored to what feels right for you. There's never just one way to do this type of work—after all, you are working in the mystical arts, which are quite different from the more exacting sciences. Be bold. Explore different types and scenarios until you find that one that feels just right for you.

If you don't wish to explore a spiritual path to connect in this manner with your dreams, you can skip the step of connecting with a spirit guide. Just create a private space in your meditation where you are inviting your superconscious mind to engage with you in order to help use a greater portion of your mind to figure out new ideas and inspired solutions to your problems.

You don't have to engage with anyone at all when setting your space. Remember, my husband preferred his communications to come from a computer screen he created in his space, similar to typing questions into Google and receiving replies.

In any case, it's helpful to establish these rituals. They set the tone and program the mind to focus the subconscious, conscious, and superconscious minds to work together and do what you are asking them to do. Over time, these exercises become commonplace to you and your mind, and it becomes quicker and easier to go into this mode and connect.

Tip 7: Create a special section in your workbook for teaching dreams.

At this point, your dream journal is really turning into a dream workbook. In it, you should create a section called "Teaching Dreams," where you describe your sacred space and note how many times a week you entered in meditation and began this exercise. Make note of how many weeks it took before you could easily create this space in active meditation, and practice creating it before you go to sleep at night. Then make note of how many weeks you practiced this exercise before sleep until you could remember the answers in your dreams.

A separate section should detail the answers you received to your questions. Note the way in which the answers were revealed. Did they come through the active meditation, in the dream sequences, or throughout the day with signs and symbols?

When you feel that you have received enlightening information or an answer to your question, go back and look over the random dreams that you have been having and recording in the past month. Determine whether any of the random dreams you were having in which you didn't ask for guidance were also giving hints and clues to the answer you sought.

You may find that you were being guided all along in your dreams. The difference is that now you have created a direct path that works more quickly and more clearly to connect and receive answers and inspiration.

Tip 8: Use accessories to heighten your dream state.

Smell is a powerful sensory activator, and some people find that a scent helps awaken their superconscious. Think about a favorite scent that you love that triggers a memory for you. Perhaps the smell of pine or sugar cookies immediately makes you think of being a child at Christmas. Certain scents can evoke powerful memories for us in this way.

Understanding how this works, you can consciously use a particular scent to program your mind to focus on a certain thought or intention every time you smell that scent. Before going to sleep, breathe in the scent from a mist spray or sachet with a fragrance that you have chosen and say, "I will remember my dreams," "My spirit guide will help me with my dreams," or another focused intention that you'd like to create during your dreamtime.

I have a vanilla-orange scent in a jar that I like, as it is strong and makes me pay attention. I open the jar and take three deep breaths of this orange scent and then lie back in bed and prepare to talk with my guides.

Whatever type of scent you like is what will work best for you. Just pick one that you normally don't use so that this sensory trigger is only connected to the meditative practice in dreamtime. Don't use a candle because you should not light a candle before falling asleep.

If scents don't work for you (maybe they are overpowering and awaken you too much, or you have allergies and prefer not to work with a scent), then try playing music before going to sleep. Pick a song that plays for two minutes, preferably just music without vocals, as you don't want any words from a song to come into your thoughts. Classical music may work best. Set the song to play and then listen to it as you fall asleep.

A third idea is to program and use a crystal. Charge it with the intention that holding it in your hand for a moment will put you in this frame of mind.

Any item you use for meditation may work for this exercise. Other ideas are a bell, chime, or small gong to focus the mind.

Tip 9: Teaching dreams can enhance your mind–body–spirit connection.

The other exciting thing about programming your mind through teaching dreams is that once you learn how to set this in place, you can use it for other purposes.

Many people will set the tone each evening before they sleep to ask for energetic healing to come through while they sleep. They visualize this healing energy surrounding their body and working on a specific area of the body that needs healing.

If they enter their sacred space, they ask their guides specific questions about what is occurring healthwise with their physical body and what they can do to help the healing process in conjunction with the medical advice they are receiving from their doctors. Healing requests can be made for physical, mental, and emotional healing as well as healing from past-life issues and other matters of the soul.

When we sleep, we are restoring the body. When we can set a program with the intention of the superconscious and subconscious minds to work in tandem to assist in healing the mind, body, and spirit, it can help direct energy to these specific areas to be of greater help.

This can be further enhanced when awake, in the form of visualizations that focus on health and wellness.

Tip 10: If you're not ready for advanced teachings, ask for sweet dreams.

If you've recently been through a very stressful experience or time in your life, it may not be the right time to engage in teaching dreams, as you may not be ready to deal with the answers to why things happened as they did.

Instead, you can ask to have sweet dreams, dreams in which you feel safe, loved, comforted, warm, and relaxed, floating in a space with your cares removed for the moment. You can do this in your active meditation and before going to sleep.

This is helpful when you've already been practicing how to have teaching dreams and have become proficient at it. This way, when something challenging comes your way in the future, you are already skilled at knowing how to program your mind and how to connect with your guides.

Ask your guides and loved ones in spirit to come hold and comfort you in their loving energy so that you can be restored on the mind-body-spirit level.

Tip 11: This work can help you in your daily life.

Once you've activated this awakened connection with your subconscious, conscious, and superconscious minds, you can use these same techniques in your daily life as well. A fun side effect of doing this dream work is that it tends to spill over into your daily life, helping your mind be more open to new ideas.

I often set the intention before going to sleep that I'd like to awaken with inspired thoughts of what I should write about that day when I'm working on a book. When I do this, I wake up and the ideas are right there ready to pour out of me. I do my best to avoid all distractions that could pull me out of this frame of mind and get to the computer as quickly as I can so that I can open up to these thoughts and let them pour forth from my superconscious mind. When I'm in this zone, the words come flying out of me, and I can write thousands of words in a day!

Try this sometime when you're working on a specific project and see how it works for you. It's not something we can do every day, as many days we have other responsibilities and expectations to manage, but on a day when you can awaken and stay in that energetic flow, the results can be amazing.

You may find a big surge in your creative and inventive ideas and more energy to take on new projects and endeavors. You've freed your conscious mind by allowing it to let go of stress and worries that are being worked out in the dream state, so when you're awake, you're ready to explore. Because the conscious mind is no longer heavily burdened, there is space to learn new things and grow.

Where Do We Go from Here?

Now that you've been practicing how to remember your dreams and engage your subconscious, conscious, and super-conscious minds to work together, you are ready to communicate even more directly with the other side.

In this chapter, you've met and worked with a spirit guide. In the next chapter, we are going to explore what it feels like when you are visited by a loved one or other spiritual being in your dreams. I call these visitation dreams.

This is the next big step, as you are leaving an area where you had some control of what you would dream about. In visitations, you may be surprised by who has been waiting to spend some time with you from the other side. Nervous? Don't worry—I'm here with you as your travel guide to the other side. We'll take this next step together.

Five

VISITATION DREAMS

One of the most peaceful, thrilling, exciting, heart-wrenching, painful, loving, and hopeful types of dream you can ever experience is a visitation dream.

In these dreams, you're not dreaming through the subconscious or working through something from the conscious mind. Instead, the veil between the earth plane and the spirit plane has opened, and someone who has passed on to the other side comes through to be with you.

If you are psychic or a medium, you have these experiences when you are awake. You may speak with ghosts (earthbound spirits) or those in spirit who have crossed over to the other side and come back through the veil to communicate. If you are not a person who has awakened these abilities within yourself at this time, you may find that your first contact with the other side is while you are asleep. This experience at first feels like a dream, but upon waking you realize that it was not a dream at all, but rather a visitation.

The Difference between Visitation Dreams and Wishful Dreams

There are many clues that reveal the difference between a visitation and a wishful dream about being able to communicate with a loved one who has passed on. Here are some of the clues that your dream is a visitation dream:

- When you awake, you have been given information that you had no other way of knowing. The person in the dream told you where to find something you were looking for or shared information about something or someone that you were previously unaware of.
- The person in the dream gives you prophetic information about something in the future, which later comes true as they said.
- When you awake, you can still feel their energy in the room, and many times there is also a familiar scent you associated with them during their lifetime still floating in the air.
- You may also have goosebumps or other physical reactions that indicate your loved one in spirit was near.

I've experienced many situations where loved ones came to me in this type of communication. I am a psychic and medium, and many times when I am consulting with a client, someone connected to them will come through during a session.

During my sessions, I always begin with a prayer of protection and ask that only those who are for the highest and best good be able to manifest during the session. This way if someone from the other side wishes to deliver a message, I've set the intention that the information received is meant to provide help.

There have been times, though, when I have been so overcome with grief from losing someone very close to me who I love dearly that I was not ready to open up to communicate with them in this manner. I've tried it many times, and if I'm still grieving, it's too overwhelming when they come through the veil of the other side to be with me. I cry so hard, feeling them so strongly around me as they come through the veil. My pain in missing them here on the physical earth plane is so strong that I'm unable to clearly communicate at that time.

As I do with all the things I teach—how to see auras, how to be psychic, how to change your life, how to communicate with spirits and ghosts, and other metaphysical courses—I speak of them because I have experienced them firsthand in my life. Over the process of trial and error and plenty of real-world experience, I have become a good teacher and travel guide to the other side through years of work and experiences. My work began in my childhood, and I studied in my teens, later studying wisdom teachings and researching the supernatural realms and experiencing them hands-on. So when I say that I can distinguish wishful dreams and missing loved ones on the other side from having a real conversation and interaction with a loved one, while sleeping or awake, I can clearly state the difference because I have lived through both and still do.

The passing of my grandfather was very difficult for me in my preteen years. Were his to be the only loss I suffered up to this point, that would have been painful enough; I miss him greatly to this day. Yet for some reason known only to the

Divine above, my journey in this lifetime has been to experience great love and great loss. After my grandfather's passing, my father passed away when I was in my twenties, and then my mother passed away in my thirties. I remember thinking, *Now I am an orphan.* My parents, who were the anchor to who I am and who understood me best as a child, are gone. Now here in my forties, I've lost the love of my life, my husband of twenty years, and I am forever changed. I'm heartbroken as a widow. All before the age of fifty, I have become a widow and an orphan. I know what it's like to experience great loss and to wake up each morning wishing for their absence to have been a bad dream.

I've had these dreams—hopeful, wishful dreams—in which I'm speaking with my husband and saying to him what a terrible dream it was that he was gone, and I'm so relieved that it's not true. Only I wake up and experience that soul-crushing, heartbreaking pain of realizing that it is indeed true. He is no longer with me here on the earth plane, and the dream was indeed just wishful thinking and the process of grief as it tries to help my conscious mind through my subconscious mind. My heart and mind try to break it to me gently over and over again that he is truly gone and that my life, my today, my now, and my future have been completely altered. These dreams help me work through the grief, the pain, and the awful realization that my life as I knew it has been torn asunder, and there is no return to how it once was.

Those of you who have lost someone that you love dearly understand the pain I speak of, and you understand what these wishful dreams feel like.

I have tried to express this to some friends who have not lost a spouse or partner, but they can't truly understand. They compare it to the loss of a parent, but it is not the same. Your parents are your anchor, a safe place to return to when needed in life. But on some subconscious level, there is the awareness that most likely they will pass on before you do, and while you love them so greatly, your experience of growth and evolution is moving forward, out of your parents' home and on to building a new life of your own. While their presence is deeply important in your life and is a comfort, it typically is not what you build your future dreams upon. Your spouse or partner, on the other hand, is the person you are building a life with, the person you set goals with, and the person you dream of growing old with. When this person is taken from this world, you lose your true north. You become rudderless, without direction. The best way I can describe it is this: one day I was hit by a tsunami and lost everything. Since then I have been clinging to a piece of wood, drifting at sea and wondering if I should focus and swim to a certain location or let the currents take me where they may until I reach new land. As an empath with mermaid-like energy, that's how I personally process grief and my deep emotions.

Those of you who have lost a partner or spouse understand of what I speak. It is a club that no one wants to belong to, and only those who belong can understand the grief and pain. This is why it's so easy to have those wishful dreams and think that you had a visitation. However, when you have a true visitation dream, you'll know the difference. You feel the person's energy. It permeates the room, and you are filled with love and a light that clears your mind, body, and spirit in that moment.

The only pain in this experience comes afterward from missing them again.

Let me describe some visitation dreams to give you an idea of what they feel like and how they are different from wishful dreams.

Visitation to Meet Those Who Passed Before We Could Meet Them in This Lifetime

When my husband and I were first together, we talked about getting married. His parents had died early in his life as well, his mother when he was eighteen and his father when he was twenty-one. We both understood what it felt like to have lost family that we loved dearly. We were chatting about family and how we wished that they could be with us here on earth.

I didn't know much about my husband's parents. The few stories he had shared were about his life with them during his teen years up until their passing. That night after chatting about them, we lay in bed together snuggling, and I said I wished that I could have known them. As I drifted off to sleep, his mother came to me in a dream state, in an active visitation. In this visitation experience, she invited me into her home and brought me into her kitchen. She sat me down at the table there, and we proceeded to have a conversation about her and her son. At the end of the conversation, she indicated that she approved of me as his choice for a wife and was happy to see us together. I knew it was a visitation because she shared information with me that I knew nothing about, and I could clearly see the home we were in, which I knew to be my husband's childhood home rather than the home he grew up in during his teen years.

I woke from the dream and woke up my husband to tell him about the experience. One of the most wonderful things about our relationship was that we had both studied metaphysical teachings and were equally dedicated to our spiritual growth in our lives. When you have a partner who shares these beliefs and goals, it makes for an incredible relationship as you explore with each other at the mind-body-spirit level. So when I woke him up to tell him his mother had come to me in a dream, he wasn't surprised at all.

As I began to describe the dream to him, he was able to confirm that it was indeed a visitation dream. In the dream, I was in his mother's home in her kitchen, but it was not a kitchen I had ever seen. His parents had moved out of state with my husband when he was ten years old, and the only pictures of his I had seen were of the house where he had lived during his teen years.

This kitchen was from the home he lived in during his toddler and elementary-school years. I described in detail the colors and look of the kitchen, the table in it, and the very specific decor in the room. I don't know why his mother decided to have this meeting with me in the kitchen from her home when my husband was a baby, but that's what she did. Perhaps it was to send the message to my husband that the dream I had was not wishful thinking that I could speak to her but was indeed a proper visitation.

I was so happy to know that she approved of our relationship and that we were to be married. The dream was very meaningful to us and brought us great happiness.

Visitations to Deliver a Message

Another type of visitation dream is a dream in which you are given private, personal information about other people that you have no current knowledge of otherwise.

My husband's father did not appear to me at that time with his mother. He came through to me several years later to deliver a personal message for me to give to my husband, which I did. I really didn't understand what the message meant, but it had great meaning to my husband. His father's appearance in that dream was another style of visitation dream. It wasn't as engaging conversationally as it had been with his mother. When his father visited me, he announced who he was and then immediately got on with his business of telling me the information that he wanted me to relay to my husband. He didn't have much interest in speaking with me or doing much of anything else, except to make sure that I fully understood the message. He asked for a guarantee that I would deliver the message to my husband. I really had no idea what this message meant; it was family related and meant something to him. In this situation, I wasn't meant to understand the message. I was just the messenger ensured to deliver it.

Visitations Experienced by Several Dreamers at the Same Time

It is also possible for several people who are connected to experience a visitation at the same time. My father once came back in a visitation dream to send a message, and my brother, my sister, and I all experienced this visitation on the same evening. We all lived in different parts of the country and had not spoken of our father in quite some time.

When this incident occurred, it wasn't a particularly meaningful date to us personally. It wasn't near his birthday or when he passed or anything of that nature. I did note, however, that it was during a very rare planetary alignment on May 5, 2000, when the planets Mercury, Venus, Earth, Mars, Jupiter, and Saturn were positioned in a straight line with the sun, and the moon was aligned between the sun and Earth. Perhaps this alignment provided a unique veil for him to cross and to send his message to each of us at the same time. I've often wondered if others received messages from loved ones during this same planetary alignment.

My brother, my sister, and I received this unplanned communication all on this same evening, and you can imagine the surprise and shock when we called each other to share what we had experienced, only to find out that each of had the experience at the same time. It's interesting to note that while we all felt his energy and attempt to communicate, what we perceived as the message was a little different for each of us. This in some part is due to how open we were to receiving the message, how good of a receiver we were in these types of communications, and also the intention of the message that my father wanted each of us to receive.

My family has come into my dreams for visitations, but it's not very often. Loved ones on the other side often act as our guides, and we can ask them to visit us when they can. It's important to note, though, that just because we ask them to does not mean that they can, nor does it mean they can come immediately when we ask them to visit.

CRules for Communicating with CThose in the Spirit CWorld

From my experiences of being on the other side and communicating with those in the spirit world, I have learned some of the rules, though not all of them. These rules and deeper understanding of how the spirit world works and communicates will help you understand why a spirit is communicating with you in the manner that they are at the time.

Rule 1: Your loved one may look different.

Often when we see our loved one in a visitation dream, we will notice that their energy is strong and vibrant and that they look the picture of health and many times younger than they did when they passed on. For example, your grandfather may not look as old as he did when he passed. You'll still recognize him, but he'll look more around the age of forty. This is not a hard and fast rule; it seems to change. When someone passes on, they first appear in your dream at the age they were when they died, but their body is restored to good health.

For example, if their body had been injured in an accident or ravaged by disease, this will no longer be reflected in their physical appearance. If your grandfather died at the age of eighty-nine, he will still look this age, but will appear more vital without the physical degeneration he had been experiencing. Over time, though, when they appear to you in your dream years after they passed, they are restored to an age that looks between thirty-five and forty-five. This appears to be the natural state that we appear in from the other side.

If the person was very young, a child or young adult, they will first appear in their form as a child, but later, they may appear to you in the form of how they would have looked between thirty-five and forty-five years old in that lifetime. Many times this evolution occurs when this person works as a guide for you throughout your lifetime. So if your loved one appears to you in a dream and they look younger than you expected, don't be thrown off by this image. They are portraying how they look in the spirit world.

Rule 2: Those in spirit have work to do on the other side, so it may take time before they can visit you in a dream.

If we are very stressed, confused, or in great pain when we died, we go to a recovery space where there are guides who help us regain our mental and emotional faculties, working on our mind, body, and spirit so that our soul is restored. The confusion could come from having passed on in a sudden accident in which we were caught unaware of our passing. It can also occur when a person has suffered with a long illness that took a huge toll on the physical body and required strong medication to dull the pain and the mind for a long period of time. In this recovery space, the person can rest and be healed.

During the recovery time, it's rare to experience a visitation from this person in your dreams. They are under the care of their guides, who are helping them restore themselves to their full state of being, and all energy is being directed to this healing. For this reason, there is no energy available to travel through the veil to visit loved ones back on earth. This is why sometimes when we lose a loved one, we don't understand why they have not been back yet to communicate with us in our dreams when they promised that they would. Give it time. When they are able to do so, they will find a way to communicate with you in a visitation dream when asked. Many people ask just once to have a visitation dream with a loved one, and if it doesn't occur right away, they give up. Try, and if it doesn't happen, try again in one year. It's also helpful to ask for this type of communication dream during a date that is important to the person who has passed, such as their birthday, a holiday, an anniversary, or another date that has great meaning for them.

Rule 3: Due to the healing process in the spirit world, spirits can often provide information and answers they did not have when alive on earth.

Once we have been restored on the other side, we review our lifetime in its entirety. We see all the thoughts, words, and actions that we took in this lifetime and we feel the emotional energy attached to each situation. When we spoke in anger, we feel the anger as it released from us and directed to another person and how it made them feel. The same feelings are shared with us from when we sent love, hope, encouragement, and laughter.

We review our lives, seeing the big picture that makes sense of it all—why we lived how we did, why we came back as a male or female, appearing how we did physically, loving who we loved, and feeling stressed around others who were in our lives—to help us experience things on that level as well. We can make peace with it because we finally understand why everything happened the way it did and what it all meant.

Once the person has gone through this life review, when they return to communicate with you in a visitation dream, the information they can share is very clear and succinct about their entire life. They can provide answers and clarity on why they did the things they did in their physical life on earth. In these visitations, you feel the extraordinary power of their love, coming from the higher planes, and they remind you that love is the most important energy of all. In these visitations, you feel better when you awake, as if their energy has restored you on some level.

Rule 4: In the spirit world, we have access to all our lifetimes, so you may have to remind the spirit which lifetime you wish to see them about in your visitation dream.

Over time on the other side, spirits begin to disconnect from their most recent lifetime. Their emotional attachments to that lifetime begin to fade from the intensity of those experiences. They are able to review many other lifetimes and see how certain experiences and people have appeared and reappeared in their lives from one lifetime to another. They begin to see an even bigger picture of what it all collectively means. This means that the longer it has been since a person has passed on, the more energy it takes for them to connect with a specific lifetime when you ask them to visit with you in a dream. Because of this, you'll want to be very specific about who you are and in what form you remember the ancestor when you ask for them to visit.

Let me give you an example: Say that you want to meet a great-grandparent who passed away long before you were born. In your request for a dream visitation, you'll want to be specific when you send the message to meet them. It's helpful to have an article of their clothing or jewelry or another item, such as a photo, that helps them connect to the form of the specific lifetime you want to meet with. On the other side now, they remember all their lifetimes, so unless you are specific, they could appear to you in the form that they are now most comfortable in, and you may not recognize them. We all change forms from lifetime to lifetime, so unless you request to meet Great-Grandpa George in a specific lifetime, you may have the surprise of meeting him as Georgia in a female version from another lifetime. Or you may have heard stories about a very conservative uncle who passed away during a war, only to appear to you in his new favorite form as a funky musician.

Rule 5: When a spirit visits in your dream, their emotional energy will feel different.

When the person is now on the other side in their spiritual form, they are still the most attached to the people whom they were most strongly involved with from the most recent lifetime. However, their emotions are not as strong in the sense that the emotions do not overcome and overwhelm them as they do to us here on earth. On the other side, we are in a space of love and compassion and do not suffer the same emotionally as our loved ones do on the earth plane. We are no longer bound to the human body and to the way that we process emotions through the body. It is a more harmonious state of being.

When you receive a visit from a loved one in a visitation dream, you will feel this in their energy. It will be strong, and light will emanate from around them in a peaceful way.

Rule 6: Spirits in visitation dreams cannot provide the answers to everything.

Most people on the other side ask to help their loved ones who are still on the earth plane, and, when possible, they are allowed to assist as spirit guides. There seem to be rules involved with how this can proceed, however.

It appears that those in the spirit world cannot tell us what to do and are not allowed to tell us everything that will come in the future. They seem mostly to be able to offer encouragement, support, and loving energy, which at times come in visitation dreams and other times when they find a way to communicate and show a sign that they are near.

It appears that our destiny is not meant to be fully revealed; part of the journey is to have the experiences as they are meant to unfold. Go ahead and ask them anything you want, though, during a visitation dream. If they can answer your question, they will.

Rule 7: Ask clearly and directly to have a visitation dream.

Like spirit guides, our loved ones in spirit have to be asked to help us. They cannot directly approach us and interfere, except in some occasions where it seems they have been given permission to visit us to give a direct communication, such as a specific message or warning or to help comfort us.

However, there seem to be times when they are allowed to help and other times when they are not. This is why sometimes they will appear in our dreams right away when we ask and other times they are not allowed to do so.

Rule 8: Just because you ask doesn't mean you will receive a dream, but the spirit may visit you directly when you're awake.

Some loved ones go on to do other things on the other side and don't come back to visit family members. Sometimes we never know why. My grandfather, whom I was so close to and who was a powerful psychic and empath, has not come back to visit me in visitation dreams, except for one small exception, no matter how often I ask.

My mother and grandmother prayed daily for decades for him to visit them in a dream or as an apparition, and he never did for either of them. My mother visited a number of mediums, attempting to communicate with him, and none of them were ever successful in communicating with him. I've worked with many mediums, and none of them have ever been able to communicate with him either. For most of my life, I didn't understand why this communication could not be received. I prayed that my mother and my grandmother, who have both passed on, were both able to find out why when they reached the other side. Both of them have visited me in dreams since their passing, but he is never with them.

Recently, I had a visitation from my grandfather, though it was not in a dream. It was unexpected and incredible. I'll share this story with you now.

My beloved grandfather has appeared to me once in all my life since he passed. I was working with a healer who does long-distance healing, and she was working on me in a session. During this long-distance session while I was awake, he appeared to me with the spirit guides who were working on healing and restoring me.

He brought his unique color of light, which I had always seen in his aura when he was alive, and he surrounded me in this light. He looked at the spirit guides who were working on me and said to them, "She is mine, daughter, granddaughter." His voice was strong and bold and full of authority. He placed his hand over my heart chakra, and a bright symbol appeared and grew very large, expanding into a breastplate like knights used to wear.

The breastplate glowed with this color and the symbol he drew, and I am still able to see it when I scan my aura. The spirit guides who were working on me deferred to him when he appeared during the healing session, as if he was a person in charge and that a visit from him to the spirit plane that they were on was a rare visit.

What I have discerned from this experience is that there are many levels to the spiritual planes, and I have traveled through many of them in my work as a psychic and medium. Some souls work on the spiritual planes that are the most closely attached to the earth plane, and they reincarnate on earth to begin another experience, to have another lifetime on earth. These souls stay closer to the earth plane and are very connected to helping their loved ones on earth, whom they will soon be with again in an upcoming lifetime.

After seeing my grandfather in the form in which he appeared and the energy and power that he was able to direct, it's my opinion that he has moved from the spiritual plane that returns us to new lifetimes on the earth plane and has evolved into a new incarnation on a different spiritual plane, where he is not as connected to the lifetimes and souls on the earthly experience.

When he appeared during this healing session I was having, it was like seeing an otherworldly being of a different vibration and nature. I recognized him and his soul source, and the energy was incredibly strong and full of love. I don't know why he appeared at that time, placed the symbol on me, and reminded the guides working on me that I belonged to him, that I was one of his tribe. It's one of those mysteries that hopefully will be revealed to me when I review my life on the other side. In the meantime, it was wonderful to see him again for a moment and to feel his warmth and love. This was a healing that I was receiving to help me process the grief and pain of losing my husband. Of all the times in my life when I could have used his help, this indeed was the most helpful and healing time of all.

Emotional Healing and Processing of Grief through Visitation Dreams

I hope these stories are giving you some good indications of what visitations from loved ones in spirit feel like in comparison to the wishful dreams that we have of missing them.

Unlike the other style of dreams, there is little you can do to generate or control the visitation. You can ask for a visitation dream, but you have to remain open to the fact that your loved one can and will visit when they are able, and you may not have any advanced notice.

Most people report having a visitation dream after the loss of someone they loved more than other time in their life. For those of you who have experienced a deep loss like this, as I have with the loss of my beloved husband, I'll share with you how intense this experience can be.

When my husband first passed, his spirit was around me everywhere. It held me like a warm blanket, as he did what he could to see me through the terrible shock. His spirit was so strong that other family members also experienced his presence during this time. He also sent out messages to many psychics and mediums that we knew, and they all reached out to me to share that he had visited them and wanted them to deliver a specific message to me. He stayed with me in this manner for close to three months. When the grief would consume me and I couldn't move or do anything but cry, he would come, and I would feel this warm, loving energy that gathered around me. It was like being held by him—warm, like a blanket of air that covered me and helped absorb and release some of the pain. Over time it stopped, as it needed to, because I longed for that feeling to be with me every day, and I didn't want to do anything else but lie down and feel his energy in this way.

He then moved from this energy work to appearing to me directly. I was not ready yet for this experience, to see him and hear him while being unable to touch him or be with him. The pain from my heart was unbearable. Our guides separated us for a while at this time, and when I pushed through the astral planes to go see him, they had guides who were guards at the door and would not let me see him. As I grew stronger emotionally, they then allowed me to see him, without him seeing me in return. At this stage, I was able to see the work he is doing on the other side, how much he is enjoying it, and how happy he is. This brought me great comfort. Now the pain I experience is just my grief at missing him in my life here on earth while knowing that he is there on the other side doing many things that he loves. I know that when I cross over at my time, that he will be there to greet me and bring me over.

As more time has passed now, we are able to converse again, and this process first began through visitation dreams. I think both of our guides wanted to make sure that it wouldn't be overwhelming again for the both of us. When we would first meet like this, I would fight to stay over there, and he would fight to stay with me here on the earth plane. We both wanted to be with each other so much, and they did not want this to continue in this manner. So the visitation dreams were a way for us to begin to communicate, and that has progressed now to being able to tell him things in this dream state so that he can communicate with me on the earth plane. I've given him specific examples of signs to send to me to communicate different answers.

We are in the process of creating a language in this way, delivering messages back and forth to each other not just in the dream state, but when I'm awake as well. It takes less energy to communicate in this way than it does when he appears before me. Now that I am clearer emotionally and don't burst completely into tears every time I feel his energy, I have more focus and can communicate with him in a more direct, conscious level.

We've also noticed there are times that, when I travel to see him on the other side, there are others around who want to monitor our communication. Again, it appears to be some of these rules that are in place on the other side, and I don't have complete understanding of how they work. I do know that over time as I get stronger, if there's a way to expand the communication, we will do it, as it is something that we are both very passionate about. We have spent many lifetimes working together on our spiritual exploration and evolution. This was not our first lifetime together, and our work continues to this day.

As a psychic medium, my process of dealing with my grief is a different experience than most people have. I share it here with you so you can understand my perspective, how grief differs for so many people, and how visitation dreams can bring peace and soulful healing. Many of you reading this book are psychics or mediums and have been exploring this work through my book *The Awakened Psychic* and may wish to attempt more direct communication like I mentioned in this story.

Interesting Things to Note When Loved Ones Visit in Dreams

You may not have a personal experience at this level with a loved one who has passed on like I described above, but they are still there for you, watching over you and sending their love and care. If you are ready to communicate with them, visitation dreams are one of the most peaceful ways to begin a conversation with loved ones.

When you go to sleep, ask them to visit you in your dreams and to tell you something about someone or something that you definitely do not know. You will then have the opportunity to confirm this information so that you will have evidence that proves to you that they did visit you from the spirit world.

There are certain times of the year when the veil between worlds is thinner and you can more easily reach through the veil to ask loved ones to visit with you in your dreams. During this three-day period, October 30 through November 1, many people choose to connect with their loved ones from the other side. One of the ways to reach out and connect with your loved ones in spirit is to host what is described as a "dumb supper." The word "dumb" in this context refers to its earlier meaning of "silent" or "mute." Silence is observed during this dinner, and people sit quietly and reflect and honor those who have gone on to the other side. It also allows for information to come through from the spirit world. The loved one is invited through the veil to come through and join this special dinner held in their honor. Once you conclude the dinner and go to bed that evening, ask the loved one to continue this conversation with you in your dreams.

Remember, like I mentioned earlier, most times when loved ones visit, they don't look exactly the same as they did when they died. They look stronger, brighter, healthier. They usually appear to be between the ages of thirty-five and forty-five, looking their absolute best, even better than they looked at that age. They glow with vitality and spiritual light. If they don't appear to you in this form, or if they appear sad and stressed, then you are probably just having a dream about them rather than being visited by them in spirit.

When you awake from a visitation dream, you are filled with love and warmth and are glowing from the peaceful and positive energy. This is the experience 99 percent of the time. I say 99 percent because I have heard stories from others who had visits from those in spirit who came to settle some unfinished business with them and were putting pressure on them to do the right thing. These dreams were tough on them. They weren't cruel, but they were enlightening. The best example of this type of dream might be the visits of the Ghosts of Christmas Past, Present, and Future who visit Scrooge in *A Christmas Carol*. These spirits show the person how life may end up if they don't make some changes. I've never experienced a visitation dream in which the spirit was anything but loving and full of light, but I can't discount the people who share that they have experienced something different in this way. I will say that it's not typical, as usually visitations are meant to encourage and support.

Visitation dreams are usually pretty specific. The loved one in spirit speaks to you directly or sends energy directly to you. In regular dreams, the people in the dream often appear and disappear in a haphazard way, which can be very confusing and difficult to understand. Visitation dreams are very closely focused on the loved one in spirit and their being with you in that moment.

On the rare occasion that a being of dark energy is attempting to look like your loved one, you'll easily notice this, as they may look like the person, but something is off. The energy feels awkward and weird, and they don't know the right things to say or the exact mannerisms that your loved one used. This is a rare occurrence, but if this happens, immediately surround yourself in white light and banish this being away forever. State that only those beings from the highest and best spiritual planes may visit you in your dream state.

If you're a person who typically doesn't remember your dreams, the visitation dream will feel larger than life and will stick with you. Fragments of this dream will pop up throughout your day, and other signs of communication will come

forth throughout the day to help jog your memory of the experience until you receive the full message. While most of us
forget our dreams, which is why we keep dream journals to
help us remember, most people never forget a visitation dream.
It is so real and poignant that it stays with us forever.

Enjoy these visitations. They are gifts from spirit, allowing
us to see a glimpse of the other side. During these visitations,
we can see that our loved ones are doing well and that they are
happy.

It's a wonderful reminder that we will see them again and
that they are not dead. Rather, they have simply shifted into
another energetic state, reminding us that life goes on and on
and on.

Six

LUCID DREAMING

Lucid dreaming is a concept that not everyone is familiar with. In any given conversation I have throughout the day, someone might ask me what's new, and I might reply, "I had a great time lucid dreaming last night." They most likely will have no idea what I'm talking about or, worse, they will jump to the wrong conclusion.

In brief, lucid dreaming means being aware that you are dreaming. A part of your consciousness remains active and is able to observe the dream you are having. Once you can observe your dreams as they are occurring, the next step is to take action in the dreams and alter them at will.

When I teach this technique to my students, I describe this as the tip of the iceberg in beginning to understand self-observation, self-awareness, and introspection. Others might describe it as slipping down the rabbit hole. Questions begin to arise: Who am I? Which conscious or unconscious part of me is actually running this show, both in my dreams and in my daily life?

What Happens in a Lucid Dream?

When you lucid dream, you can change the dream, stop the dream, and make yourself wake up from the dream. You can add people or animals and change the scene of the dream. In this dream state, if you don't like where the dream is going or how people are acting in it, you can change this too. It's like being the ultimate director and producer of your own personal movie. Yeah, it's pretty cool.

Monks, yogis, shamans, and almost all types of spiritual wisdom teachers have taught how to lucid dream for as far back as we can trace in these ancient forms. They have used different terminology to describe these dreams, but the results were the same. I'm surprised this technique isn't taught more by psychologists, as it provides a way to work out one's problems by trying out multiple scenarios in the dream sequence. It provides the opportunity to see how things play out and how you feel in each different scenario. After all, it's like daydreaming in your sleep.

Some people experience their first lucid dream accidentally, and it's a shock to them. They may have a dream in which they are experiencing a stressful situation, such as falling off a tall building or feeling out of control in a scary situation, and in their panic, they scream "Stop!" and put their hands out. To their great surprise, the dream freezes to a halt, as if the dreamer had a remote control in their hands and paused the television from playing. If they are aware that this is a lucid-dream moment, they may then play around, lowering their body safely to the ground, removing an object they don't like from the dream, or removing a person from the dream sequence.

As I'm describing what this looks and feels like, I realize that for many people, playing video games can be similar to this experience, as the player chooses their character, runs through different scenarios, and removes other players and objects from the game at times.

In the early days of lucid dreaming, most people enjoyed flying, feeling invincible, or being able to control their environment. These things are great fun, but the greater purpose of lucid dreaming is to help you get in touch with what's going on in your life on a deeper conscious and subconscious level in order to explore new directions that you can take in your life.

The Point of Lucid Dreaming

Lucid dreaming can help you face your fears and can also be a great stress reliever, even helping to soothe hurt feelings from the past. For example, let's say that yesterday you had a stressful encounter with another person and you didn't handle it as well as you could have. Perhaps you acted bluntly and rudely and said things that you shouldn't have said. In your lucid dream, you can recreate this encounter and run through the scenario, practicing how you would handle this type of situation should it happen again in the future. This can help you work through the emotional process and feel more confident about your ability to not fly off the handle the next time you interact with this person or situation.

As you continue to practice lucid dreaming, you can incorporate it with your spiritual connection. For example, let's say there's a person to whom you wish you could say things, and for whatever reason you can't currently say this to them. Maybe this person has passed on to the other side, you have no idea where to find them now, you are estranged from them, or it would not be a good thing to interact with them in person. In your lucid dream, you can create a scenario in which you can speak with this person's soul/higher self.

You design a location where the two of you meet higher self to higher self, and you say what you have always wanted to say to this person. Then with the intentions of greatest good, you send this message to this person's higher self, imagining them receiving this information.

Depending on how intuitive this other person is, they may receive the message in a dream. Whether they are aware of the energy sent to them or not, on some energetic level it is received. Like for all practices of this kind, only send out the highest and best good energy, thoughts, and intentions, because what you send out comes back to you in energetic waves three times stronger. This is a more advanced practice in lucid dreaming that will take some time to build up to.

Frequency of Lucid Dreaming

It's not good to lucid dream too often or to recreate the same dream over and over. There are advanced esoteric wisdom teachings that explain "thought forms": if we focus on one thing for too long, we can create this image into being in the astral planes, and over time it can manifest onto the earth plane.

In the New Age community, people are taught how to do this by focusing on a wish that they desire to manifest, for example. In lucid dreams, some people get caught up in a fantasy world of their making and create a character that is their "dream person." Should they continue to focus their energy too often on this character, it can begin to manifest in the astral realm. The astral realm is a specific spiritual plane where thoughts that are given enough energy can become things. Over time and given enough energy, this character can take form, grow, and manifest into something that will not be like what is created in the dream. This is a rare occurrence, but, nonetheless, one should know all the side effects of lucid dreaming.

Lucid dreaming at the very advanced levels is still taught by some practitioners. Dream yoga, for example, is one form of advanced lucid dreaming, taught by some Tibetan Buddhist monks. One chapter cannot begin to cover the extent of lucid dreaming. If it's something that appeals to you, I recommend seeking a teacher who can explain how this process works in great detail. Most people find the biggest advantage of lucid dreaming to be the ability to wake themselves up from a bad dream and stop the dream from returning so that they can enjoy a restful night's sleep.

As with all things, balance is the key. It's not good to lucid dream too often, as the subconscious mind also needs the opportunities to have regular dreams in order to sort out situations that occur on a daily basis.

Benefits of Lucid Dreaming

I've often been asked if lucid dreaming wears me out and if I'm exhausted when I awake, as I've been busy in my dreams doing all kinds of things.

The answer, in my experience anyway, is that it appears to have no physical effect. I feel the same as I do any other night when I sleep and don't lucid dream. Sometimes when I awake from lucid dreaming, I actually feel better because I've overcome an emotional or mental stumbling block in my dream state and feel excited and positive about what I will be doing that day.

One of the greatest benefits of lucid dreaming is that it helps you understand and work out why a dream is recurring. Have you ever had a recurring dream like the types I described in chapter 3? For many people, these typically aren't pleasant dreams. They usually focus on something disturbing: a common example is feeling scared in the dream and running away from something or someone. Sometimes you can see or hear the person chasing you; other times, you never see what is chasing you and just feel the fear and the urge to run away. In this type of dream, once you become lucid and realize that it's just a dream, you can change what's happening. Facing your fear, you can stop running and turn around and demand that the person or thing chasing you show itself and explain why it is chasing you.

How to Use Lucid Dreams to Help with Recurring Dreams

I've spoken with many people over the years who have used lucid dreaming in their recurring dreams to wonderful results. Here are some examples of their recurring dreams and what changed for them when they could lucid dream and face their fear:

Dream 1: Chased by a Wolf

In my dream, I was running from the awful sounds of a snarling animal who was huge and sounded like a wolf. When I was able to lucid dream, I stopped running, turned around, and demanded that the wolf stop and then tell me what it wanted. At this point,

*the wolf was stunned into submission. He whimpered and low-
ered himself to the ground and shrunk into the size of an adorable
puppy. I picked up the puppy and cuddled it, and it licked my face.*

*When I woke up, I looked up the shamanic meaning of a wolf in
a dream and found out what the wolf was representing for me in
this experience. Now that I understand what the wolf was trying to
tell me and why I was feeling threatened, I've never had this dream
again.*

Kala's Note

In this case, the person owed money to a friend and was worried about not being able to pay the person back in time according to the agreement they had made. In their dream, they
faced a wolf, and it changed to a loving puppy. When they
researched the meaning of the dream, they realized that the
wolf represented their fear of having to tell their friend that
they couldn't pay back the money they owed. This gave the
person the courage to call their friend and explain the situation, rather than avoid them like they had been doing.

They had been imagining in their head that their friend
would be extremely upset by this news (responding like the
wolf), but to their surprise, their friend was instead very warm
and supportive (like the puppy) and had no problem extending the deadline and the payment schedule in a manner that
the person could easily handle.

Dream 2: Hiding in the Basement

*I kept having this recurring dream in which I was in this broken-
down old house that was dark and scary. Something was chasing
me, and I would run and hide in the basement every time while it
searched for me. The next time I had this dream, instead of running*

to the basement, I asked for the person or thing to show itself to me. Rather than appearing to me, it just dissipated into nothingness, and the house was quiet and still. I then calmly walked to the front door and stepped out of the house. I've never had this dream again.

Kala's Note

This person consulted with me and for further understanding also researched the meaning of dreaming about an old scary house and going into the basement. Dreams about houses give many clues about what the person is feeling about their status and the status of others. The different levels of the house can indicate the progress that the person is making. In this case, the person was suffering from very low self-esteem, and every time a situation would get tense for them, they would have a fight-or-flight reaction, which is what we do at the root chakra level. When this dreamer felt stressed, they ran away and hid from the situation.

Once they understood that there wasn't a big bad thing coming for them—that instead it was their fear of not being able to handle things that caused this instant retreat—they were able to work on adopting new coping skills to handle conflict and stress. As they worked on gaining self-confidence, they were able to lucid dream and ask the person or thing in the dream to show itself. It dissipated into nothing, showing the person that, indeed, it was just their fear that they were running from. At this point in the lucid dream, they were able to rise from the fight-or-flight root-chakra level and leave the lowest level of the home, the basement. They "rose" to the main floor and were able to calmly and confidently walk out the front door.

Dreams in which you see yourself on a different level of a building are very important to pay attention to. You may dream about your career and see yourself on the fifth floor, when you previously worked on the third floor of the building. In the dream, you may see your coworkers on the third floor but find yourself taking the elevator and getting off on the fifth floor to go to work. This can indicate that a raise or promotion is coming your way soon. If you want to work on manifesting this promotion, you can lucid dream and see yourself getting on the elevator, which opens on the highest floor, and meeting the president or CEO of the company, who is welcoming you to your new position.

Dream 3: Embarrassed in front of Coworkers

Every time I would get to a certain point in my career where I was doing well, I would have a recurring dream that my boss brought me up to the stage during a big company meeting and gave me an award for my work. At first I was excited as I walked up to the stage, but as I got closer, I would see a disapproving look on my boss's face. As I looked out at my coworkers sitting in the seats, they were shaking their heads, and some began to boo me. Each time I have this dream, I run from the stage feeling embarrassed and looking to hide in another room.

Kala's Note

When this dream was shared with me, I was fascinated. I wish I had known the person when they were actively having this recurring dream, but when I met them, the dream had already taken place. This person was already a lucid dreamer, so when they would dream about the scenario, they would change the outcome in the dream. However, the dream continued to re-cur, and it would never be any better. In this case, it turned out to be a prophetic dream. This person's boss had it out for them and was setting them up for failure. The boss did nominate them to receive an award while knowing ahead of time that a particular project was going to be investigated and found to have caused harm to their customers. The person who had the dream did not know what was going on behind the scenes on this project and was caught off guard when they were blamed and took the fall. Now wiser from this horrible experience, they left this company and moved on to a better situation.

Facing Fears in Lucid Dreams

As you review these dream examples, can you see that the dreams are creating a scenario that helps the person work out a fear or struggle that they are experiencing?

In the third dream, the person at work is struggling with the concern that their work is not good enough or that it won't be respected by their coworkers or bosses, though they are not sure why they feel this way, since they are receiving an award for the work done. The dream is trying to help the person work through why they feel this way.

If the person could stop the dream when they get on stage, they could change the dream to get some answers. Standing on the stage, they could step up to the mic and ask their co-workers, "What do you think I could do better to help with this project?" They could also ask their boss, "What would you like me to do differently in my role at work?"

If they had asked these questions during a lucid dream, perhaps it would have been revealed to them that this was a prophetic dream. The boss might have said, "I'm going to give you all the credit on this project, no matter what happens." Or one of the coworkers in the crowd who was booing might have yelled that the project was flawed or broken or might have given some hint to what was going on in this situation.

Lucid dreaming opens the mind to exploring and possibly getting new ideas regarding the perceived problem. I am not a psychologist, but I do assist my clients in dream interpretations and the meanings of certain symbols. At the end of the session, though, I remind them that the best dream interpretations come from the individual who had the dream, as they know all that is going on in their life and why certain people, places, and experiences are showing up in their dreams.

Lucid dreaming is extremely complicated, and it can be easy to go off on a tangent, get caught up in it, and become even more confused. It's best to get some training if this is a path that you want to pursue.

Remember what I said in the beginning: it's like falling down the rabbit hole, and you have no idea where you might end up if you open this door. In a dream book, lucid dreaming has to be discussed and defined in some part, but for most people, it's something that is best done not too often.

It's interesting and exhilarating to lucid dream, but like all things, moderation is key. It wouldn't be a good to lucid dream too often, as it could throw off your regular dream cycles and scenarios, which are important to give your conscious, subconscious, and superconscious minds the opportunity to work out things in the manner needed to do so. There is some fascinating research on lucid dreams, but there is still a great deal more to understand.

Falling through the Rabbit Hole of Lucid Dreaming: My Eye Color Exploration

Okay, so that heading can sound a bit intimidating when we look at all the quirky places that lucid dreaming can take us. Really, though, for most intents and purposes, lucid dreaming can be a helpful tool when used wisely to overcome a problem that's troubling you.

I remember many of my lucid dreams and how empowering they feel, especially in the knowledge that I am no longer at the whim of whatever bad dream I might experience. When I first began to understand that I was lucid dreaming, I decided in that state to program my mind and my higher self to remember how to lucid dream again, so that I could call upon this action anytime I felt uncomfortable in a dream. I also set the program so that any time I have an upsetting dream, I can call forth the action to either wake up or go into the lucid dream state so that I can continue to dream but be in better control of how the situation progresses.

Through lucid dreaming, I've had some very interesting adventures. Here's one of the most fascinating lucid dreams that I've ever experienced:

In my early thirties when I was studying how to lucid dream, I began to practice with it to see what all was possible. The thing is, no one really knows the extent of what is possible and what the dreams can lead to. This is one of the unknown mysteries and adventures that we are still exploring.

I was trying all kinds of metaphysical adventures and explorations back then, wanting to grab it all like a kid in a candy store. It was a fun and wild time, and part of the fun was that my husband was also into all these teachings as well, so we could explore them together and compare notes after our return journeys from things like astral travel, astral projections, and lucid dreams.

As I grew more confident in my abilities with lucid dreaming, I began to wonder if I could do something in my dreams that would eventually manifest into the physical earth plane. As I mentioned earlier, when doing this type of work, there is some concern about turning thought forms into thought beings, so I decided to stay away from it.

Instead, I wondered if I could change something about myself personally through the power of lucid dreaming. I had been reading *Autobiography of a Yogi* around that time and was fascinated with what could be achieved through the practice of mindfulness.

I thought about what I could try to do in my dream, and I wanted it to be something that would be noticeable, a change that people could see on my physical body, not just feel energetically around me. I'm a redhead with hazel eyes, which means they have brown and green colors mixed in them. Most people notice that my eyes change color slightly depending upon the color shirt that I'm wearing. Overall, my eyes look more hazel-brown. So I wondered, could I make my eyes look greener?

I began a series of exercises in which I would lucid dream, and each time I would see another me standing with her back to me. I would call my name out loud and as she turned around, I would look at her eyes, looking at me, and they would be a bright, beautiful green. I continued this exercise for six weeks, never telling anyone what I was doing. About a month into this practice, my close friends began to comment to me that my eyes were so green and that they had never noticed it before. My husband remarked on this many times, as did other friends and associates. It was exciting, and each time someone mentioned it, I would go to a mirror to see how green my eyes were looking that day.

After about six weeks, I got sidetracked. It was such a busy time in my life then that after long days, I was so tired at night that I was just grateful to fall into bed and pass out. I had no energy to even think about trying to lucid dream. I know many of you reading this can relate—we all want to explore our spiritual practices and do things like setting aside time to meditate or do yoga or put something new that we've learned into daily practice, but as the old saying goes, life is what happens when you're busy making plans. I was a busy mom and wife and working and doing all the things that go with family life.

About three months later, I finally felt things had calmed down enough that I could go enjoy a dinner out with my girlfriends, so I called them up and arranged a date. It had been so long since we had seen each other, and we were all looking forward to an evening out to catch up on each other's lives. Sitting down at dinner, someone asked me what was new, and as I started talking, one of the girls interrupted me and said, "Are you wearing contacts?"

Shocked, I said, "No, I'm not wearing contacts. I've never worn contacts. I don't even wear glasses. Why in the world are you asking me if I'm wearing contacts?"

"Your eyes aren't green anymore. They're hazel."

The other girls then were all studying my eyes and saying, "Yeah, your eyes are green. How did they change to hazel-brown?"

Here's the really interesting thing: I had known these women for several years, and they were now at this dinner, all pretty convinced that my eyes had always been green. They were now confused about why my eyes were hazel-brown with only small flecks of green.

I should explain at this point that in my twenties and early thirties, I rarely discussed my metaphysical training and explorations with friends where I lived. I was living in a Bible Belt area of the United States, where people who were not fundamentalist Christians were bullied and treated poorly. It took me a while before I opened up and shared my psychic abilities with my friends in this area, and this experiment happened before I began to write and teach publicly.

So here I was at this dinner with my girlfriends, who had no idea that I had ever done anything metaphysical in nature. They didn't know I been reading tarot cards and doing astrology charts since the ages of twelve and thirteen. They didn't know I saw auras, had prophetic dreams, and did psychic readings over the phone for clients in other parts of the world. They knew me only as a wife, a mother, and a fun girlfriend who liked to spend time with them.

Now they were looking at me very confused, all ready to swear that I'd always had green eyes, and they couldn't understand why my eyes were hazel-brown now.

I was amused and not quite sure what to say, as I was not ready yet to reveal who I was and the things I did, like lucid dreaming. They were all staring at me now and looking into my eyes, and I realized that it had been several months since I'd done any lucid dreaming.

I guessed the effect of my eyes looking greener only lasted for a short period of time, back when I was focused on this in my dreams, which was the last time they had seen me. I thought about my eyes looking so green back then, and I loved how they looked. I could see this beautiful green color in my mind. I said to my friends, "I know, I love when my eyes are green." As I said this to them, I was picturing how my eyes look so vibrantly green in my lucid dreams.

My friends gasped and pulled back a bit in their seats, some putting their hands over their mouths in surprise. "Your eyes just flashed bright green for a minute, really bright, and now they are back to hazel-brown. What is going on with you?"

I was fascinated, realizing that when I tapped into the psychic energy and memory of my lucid dream, I somehow manifested this energy in this moment and briefly returned my eyes to green. I didn't know how in the world to explain this to my friends. I gave them a flimsy excuse that I was experiencing some hormonal changes in my body. What they didn't buy, however, was how my eyes had just flashed so brilliantly green. I tried to laugh it off and joke about how many drinks they must have had before I arrived tonight and quickly moved on to a different subject.

When I returned home, I shared the story with my husband and asked him if he'd noticed that my eyes were no longer green. He admitted that things had been so hectic with work and everything else that was going on in our lives at the time that he hadn't gazed into my eyes in a while to even notice. Looking now into my eyes, he agreed that they were hazel-brown with flecks of green. Unlike the girls at dinner, he remembered the color of my eyes always being hazel. He asked me to try and flash my eyes green like I did at dinner with the girls, and I tried but it did not happen. I'm mystified why it happened in front of my friends but not again.

Over the next couple of weeks, I thought about my flashing green eyes, but I didn't try lucid dreaming again during this time. One night around this time, I decided that my husband and I were long overdue for a romantic date night. I made reservations for us and got dressed up for the evening, including some sexy lingerie that I'd be revealing later that night when we returned home.

After a wonderful dinner and conversation, we were back home and preparing for bed. He was lying on the bed, and I came out of the master bathroom wearing my lingerie and feeling sexy and powerful and womanly. He was smiling at me, and I was feeling great. I posed and started slowly walking toward him with passion in my eyes as I held his gaze.

"Oh my god," he said, and I thought, *Wow, this lingerie is worth every penny I spent.* I had no idea his reaction would be this great. He reached out and pulled me over onto the bed. He was gazing into my eyes, and I thought about how I was so in love with this man. My emotions were washing over me, and I was completely caught up in the romance of the evening and the love, passion, and desire that I felt for him.

It was then that I realized he was still just gazing into my eyes and hadn't made any other moves. In fact, he was not really gazing passionately like I was—he was just staring into my eyes, scanning them like a scientist might.

"What is it?" I asked, sitting up a little bit. "Why are you staring at me like that?"

He was still looking into my eyes, and finally he said, "When you walked into the room and looked at me, your eyes flashed a brilliant green color. It's like nothing I've ever seen, except maybe in a sci-fi movie."

Great, I thought, *I'm trying to take one night to be a romantic femme fatale and instead I end up being something out of a sci-fi flick.* This was not exactly where I wanted this night to go. My husband, on the other hand, was completely fascinated. Have I mentioned that he was not exactly the romantic type by nature? He was an engineer who loved to research and dissect things, and I'd just become his new subject of interest.

He was sitting across from me on the bed, holding my arms and saying, "Do it again, do it again."

"I don't know how," I replied. "I don't know how I did it either time, at the restaurant with the girls or here with you. Even worse, I don't even know I'm doing it when I do it."

This triggered a lengthy discussion between the two of us, as we were both researchers and scholars of spiritual work as well as practitioners, and we were trying to understand how this effect could occur through lucid dreaming. We went over every inch of my work, starting with the first time I decided to lucid dream about having green eyes. My husband created a chart on the computer to analyze all the data, and we continued going over the details long into the night. It was not quite the romantic night I envisioned, but it was still incredibly sexy in its own way, as we were soul mates, exploring all sides of each other on the mind-body-spirit level.

We finally concluded that when I was feeling very excited in some way, such as when I was with a group of people in a happy conversation or in the throes of passion with my man, it somehow activated the touchstone of this energy that I was building in my lucid dreams and created the effect of my eyes turning brilliant green. We determined that because I was no longer lucid dreaming or working in any way when awake either to attempt to manifest my eyes to look more green, my eyes have returned to their regular color. However, when my emotional energy field in my aura was highly excited, I appeared to be tapping into those spiritual fields and creating in a flash of light the energy memory of the green eyes.

This led to some incredibly fun research in which my husband explored different techniques to arouse my passion in order to see my eyes flash green again. Those stories, though, are definitely meant for a different type of book.

If you're wondering, I never tried to lucid dream my eyes into turning green again. While it was fascinating, I worried that I didn't have enough information to know what to do if something stranger began to happen. I wondered, for example, what would happen if I continued and my eyes started flashing like that throughout the day. I also didn't know the long-term ramifications of doing this or if I would have any control over the effects. After all, I wasn't able to control the green flashing when I was overcome with an excited or passionate emotion.

In time the flashing calmed and then stopped, as I never put any further conscious energy into making my eyes turn green again. Over the years, however, I have noticed that in some very intense emotional experiences, my eyes will still turn green, beginning with a small, less intense flash. This occurs when I am very happy or excited about something. One of my theories for the power of this particular lucid dreaming exercise is that many times when I have dreams of my most recent past lives, I see myself with green eyes. It feels almost foreign to me in this lifetime to have the hazel-colored eyes that I do.

I think that is part of why it was so easy for me to tune in to changing my eyes during lucid dreaming and why the flashing of green would occur when I was highly emotionally charged.

How to Try Lucid Dreaming for Yourself

Step 1: Consciously State That You Want to Lucid Dream

Before going to sleep, announce to yourself that tonight you want to be consciously aware in your dreams so that you are truly aware when you are dreaming. This conscious statement programs the mind to do your bidding. It's best to try this for the first time on a night when you are not too tired; otherwise, you will sleep so deeply that it's hard to rouse yourself out of your sleep cycle.

Step 2: Describe Your Desired Dream

Now that you've told your mind that you want to lucid dream tonight, specifically describe what type of dream you want to have and what you want to do in the dream. For example, you might say, "Tonight I want to dream that I'm in a jungle. As I'm walking through the jungle, I will meet an elephant. The elephant will be friendly and offer me a ride. I will ride on this elephant and travel through the jungle."

Step 3: Plan an Action That Announces Your Awareness

The next command to set in your mind is that you will do something that announces to your unconscious mind that you are aware that you are dreaming and that when you do this act, your subconscious, superconscious, and conscious minds will all become aware that you are aware you are dreaming. One example is to clap your hands every time you realize you are in a dream. Or you might wave your hands, stomp your feet, or whistle or sing a particular song. It doesn't matter so much what act you do. What matters is that it is always the same act and remains consistent.

Step 4: Observe the Dream

Once you become aware that you are in a dream and you engage in the act that announces that you are aware of the dream and are now lucid dreaming, you will be watching the dream continue around you. It's like stepping into a TV show, where you are often the star of the show. At first, you may just want to watch the dream unfold, paying closer attention to what's happening in the dream while programming your mind to remember all the details when you awake.

Step 5: Make a Small Change

When you are comfortable observing as a lucid dreamer, the next step is to change something in the dream. In the elephant-riding dream example, you might change the shirt that you are wearing from green to pink or add a beautiful headdress to the elephant. Start with a small change like this to get comfortable with making changes in your dreams.

Step 6: Stop the Dream

Now that you can make small changes, you can practice stopping the dream, which really is making the conscious decision to freeze the dream. At this point, you can program your mind to wake you up from the dream, or you can choose to stay in the dream and change the outcome. In the elephant dream, you can have the elephant turn around and take you somewhere new, or the elephant could turn into a giant tiger that you are now riding around in the jungle.

Step 7: Test Different Outcomes

As you become more comfortable with lucid dreaming, begin to incorporate real-world scenarios into your dreams. Follow the previous steps; state what the dream will be about, and then go into the dream and try different outcomes to this situation. Some examples are choosing between two careers or deciding how serious you are about the person you are dating. In the lucid dream, create a day at each of the career choices so that you can experience which job feels right to you. Spend a day with the person you are dating and try out different scenarios to see how it feels when you are with them.

Seven

NIGHTMARES

Nightmares. An old meaning of this word refers to entities from the spirit world who eat energy to survive. Because of their lower-level energetic vibration, these dark beings like to eat negative energy full of anger and fear, so they attempt to affect their victim's dreams and turn them into unpleasant situations. They drift around at night looking to find someone sleeping so they can take their energy without them knowing. As a person dreams of something unsettling, their emotional field begins to release the energy of fear and anger and other sad emotions. The entity scoops up this energy and eats it while the dream continues, riding the energy waves released by the dreamer for as long as they can.

Some old European legends believed to be from the sixteenth century say that this type of malevolent spirit includes the incubus (male) and succubus (female), both creatures that reportedly grabbed your hair in order to hang on while they rode your dreams. Some people believed back then that if you woke up the next morning and your hair was especially tangled and messy, a spirit of this type had caused this entanglement. They also believed that the incubus and succubus could encourage a person to dream about sexual activity so they could absorb the waves of sexual energy rising from the person during their dreams.

Some people wake from a bad dream with the feeling that there was a negative entity in the room around them while they were dreaming. While we describe any type of bad dream as a nightmare, very few nightmares are caused by a hungry spirit. In reality, these are very rare. Most nightmares are part of daily life dreams, through which we are working on our problems and concerns.

Feeling Something around You When You Sleep

I teach my students psychic self-defense to help protect them in their daily life and in their dream state. This is helpful, as some dream practitioners like to engage in advanced practices, which can include astral traveling in their dreams. As they travel to the different planes in spirit world, it's a good practice to ensure that they return from their travels with only the purest and highest energy surrounding them. The easiest way to keep a force field of protection around you is to surround yourself in the white-light field around your body, which I shared in chapter 1.

However, there is a simple way to test if any type of entity has come around when you were asleep. This is a very old tradition. Here's what to do:

Step 1: To ensure that no negative forces have been around you during your sleep, place a glass of spring or artesian water on the nightstand before you go to bed.

Step 2: In the morning when you wake, take two sips of the water. If the water tastes normal, all is well.

Step 3: If there is a bitter or acidic taste to the water, pour the rest of the water down the drain and surround your body in the white-light force field. Once this field is around your body, see the field expand until the white light fills the entire bedroom. Visualize the light clearing all the energy from the room. Continue expanding this powerful white-light shield outward from your bedroom until it surrounds your entire home. State out loud while doing this that nothing of a lower vibrational level can remain around you or in your home and that only beings of the highest and best vibration are welcome.

Again, this is a very rare occurrence. The old stories about nightmares come from a time when people did not fully understand how the conscious and unconscious mind operate to help us work through problems in our dreams.

Typically, this type of test and protection is only for advanced practitioners who are actively engaging in traveling to the various astral and spiritual planes through their dreams and sometimes need to do a cleansing checkup afterward.

How Nightmares and Dreams Affect Us When We Sleep

To understand nightmares in general, we have to first understand what happens when we sleep. Each sleep cycle is important for the mind, body, and spirit. As we discussed earlier, sleep helps us work out our thoughts and emotions from daily experiences as well as travel to the other planes to communicate with the other side.

Sleep also allows the brain to sort out everything that we learned and encountered throughout each day—good, bad, and neutral. As we sleep, the brain sorts through all this information. It decides what is important and needs to be saved and stored, which we then refer to as a memory. It discards some data that was gathered that day that seems irrelevant and files the other experiences in the appropriate areas so that we can retrieve them at will.

Our brain is like a huge computer collecting and processing information so that we can use this information to help us in our lives. Just like our work on a computer, sometimes we browse the web, look at information, and move on to something else. Other times we bookmark this information to return and look at again at a later time. Some information we document, write down, and record so that we can refer to this material anytime we want.

We do this same action with our mind. We absorb information and store it, which we call learning something. When we sleep at night, our mind does a backup of the important data, just like we back up information on the hard drive of our computer. Some data we store in our higher-self consciousness, where it's accessible in the global consciousness and on the other side. This is like storing data from our computers in the cloud.

Each bit of information and experience that we learn from helps us grow and evolve, taking that knowledge gathered and turning it into wisdom that we've gained. It's really an amazing course of action of how we process and work at the mind-body-spirit level of connectivity.

In addition, while all this massive data collection and sorting is occurring each night, each sleep cycle is also allowing the body the time to repair and restore itself, which is why we are advised to sleep and rest for long periods of time when we are not feeling well. A good night's sleep is so important because it allows us to sort through and release the stresses from the day. If we sleep well, we awake refreshed and revitalized, ready to face a new day, and we immediately begin to gather data and sort through it as soon as we wake up, including instantly noticing how light or dim it is outside, how warm or cool the temperature is, and what's going on in our immediate surroundings.

Next, our thoughts kick in about what we need to do right away: get ready for work or school, wake the children—all the millions of bits of data that we process on a daily basis. At this point, many of us haven't even gotten out of bed yet to start the day!

Holistic healers in ancient times would begin to treat a patient with a medical condition by sitting with the patient overnight and watching over them as the person slept and dreamed. When they noticed that the person was dreaming, they observed the process. When it appeared that the dream was over, they would gently wake the person and ask them what they had dreamt about while it was fresh in their mind. The clues provided by the patient from these dreams, especially their nightmares, often indicated what was going on with the person on the emotional and mental level. These dreams provided information about why the person was feeling stressed and ill at ease, which can contribute to physical illness in the body.

Most nightmares come from the worries that we carry with us into bedtime. As we are subconsciously sorting through this data of information that recently happened to us, some experiences have a stronger, more disturbing effect on us.

When we are in the deepest part of REM sleep, we dream, which is how we work through these thoughts and things in the subconscious and conscious minds that have been affecting us in some way. Some nightmares are not data driven; rather, they occur when we are physically ill or feverish, as the body is diverting all of its energy into healing. Nightmares can also be caused by eating too close to bedtime. When the stomach has to work overtime to digest food late at night before bed, it can cause unsettling dreams. This can especially be a problem with greasy food like pizza or heavy food like burgers.

Recurring Nightmares and Night Terrors

The most disturbing nightmares don't seem to be the ones people described in the old days as caused by an incubus or succubus. Rather, the most troubling are the recurring nightmares.

Some recurring nightmares are trying to send us a message, which we've discussed in the prophetic dreams chapter, chapter 3. There are also recurring nightmares, which are part of a daily life dream situation and which many times are caused by deep anxiety and stress related to a traumatic event in a person's lifetime. High-stress events and PTSD are related to these types of dreams. The dreams can escalate from nightmares into what are described as night terrors, in which the person can act out while dreaming, moving around the bed, waving their arms and legs, punching, and speaking out loud. Night terrors continue as a type of recurring dream and can escalate during times of stress and anxiety in a person's daily life.

Unlike a typical nightmare, which occurs and rarely happens again, night terrors continue to come to the person. In these cases, seeking the assistance of a psychologist is helpful to the person and allows them to release the emotional energy attached to the situation that is causing them the anxiety so that they can work it out in the conscious mind, which in turn helps the subconscious mind with its work in the dream state. The mind, body, and spirit are a very complex system of connections between the earth plane and the spirit planes, and we still don't fully understand how it all operates on these levels.

In the case of night terrors, sleep studies have shown that they typically occur during a non-REM pattern of sleep when the person is transitioning from one sleep state to another. When we are having a dream or a regular nightmare, we are in deep REM sleep, and the body is prepared for dreamtime. Our brain sends signals to temporarily paralyze our muscles so that we don't move during this stage of sleep. This is a nightly process in which the brain helps the body through the dream process.

During this sleep cycle, we stay in one position in order to keep our physical body from acting out the dream. This is why when you wake up from this deep stage of sleep with your dream on your mind, you also notice that you feel the need to change positions in bed. You may feel that you need to stretch, and maybe you even drooled on your pillow. Imagine if our brains didn't keep our bodies from moving during these dreams—we could be running around the house and acting out all types of scenarios in our dreams every single night.

Sleep Paralysis

Many people ask me about a frightening condition called sleep paralysis, which is very different from the temporary muscle freeze of the nightly deep REM sleep cycle. In the deep dream sleep cycle, you are not aware of your physical body at all or that it is temporary paralyzed. If you wake up during this cycle, you feel disoriented, and it takes you a minute to feel fully conscious, but you are able to move your body instantly like normal.

In sleep paralysis, it is the opposite experience. The person wakes up mentally and is fully conscious, but they are unable to move their physical body, which is understandably a very frightening experience. You feel trapped in your body with no way to communicate to anyone else that you are awake.

Many people who have experienced this in the past didn't understand what was going on with the body, and they feared that a supernatural being was holding them down and paralyzing them. I'm not saying that this may not be the case sometimes, as there are thousands of reports of alien visitations in which people report this happening to them and watching the alien in their room. I have never had an experience of this kind, so I only know what others have reported. My experiences have more to do with entities in the spirit world, and I have found that while they can be in the room and try to suck energy that is released from each of us, like an incubus or succubus, they don't seem to be able to forcibly hold our body down in what I have experienced and studied.

Sleep researchers report that when sleep paralysis occurs, the body continues to operate and function with breathing and the heart pumping, but for a few awkward and scary moments (up to several minutes), the body is stuck in a paralyzed state until the brain reconnects and notices that the person has woken up and that the muscles in the body need the ability to move freely again.

Returning to the computer analogy, this phenomenon reminds me of when my computer is backing something up while I'm trying to work. If I move the mouse to perform an additional action, the computer can freeze up for a second as it tries to simultaneously respond to me as well as back up information.

If you ever experience sleep paralysis, try your best to remain calm. It helps to focus on trying to move any tiny part of your body: try wiggling your fingertips or toes at first. Small responses like this will be possible first, and then the rest of your free body movement will be restored. But don't worry about this too much; it's a rare occurrence.

Eight

SLEEP WALKING AND SLEEP TALKING

Sleep walking and sleep talking are different from night terrors and nightmares.

When a person is sleep walking or sleep talking, they typically have no memory of having done so, though they may remember their dreams when they wake up. Studies have shown that this happens more to children, though for some it does continue into adulthood.

Sleep Walking

For a period in my childhood, I was a sleep walker. No one knows how often this occurred, as I have no memory of it except for one occasion, and unless someone else was awake and saw me, my family had no idea of how often this was happening.

I remember only one experience, and that is because I was woken up while sleep walking. I was at my grandmother's house and sleeping with her in her bedroom. She and my grandfather slept in separate bedrooms, as is the custom for some couples as they get older. Her bedroom was at the front of the house and had a door that led outside to the front porch. Back in those days, many homes in the South had access to porches from the bedrooms, as not everyone had air-conditioning. On hot summer nights some people would sleep on the porch to enjoy the cooler night air.

On one of these nights at my grandparents' home, I sleep walked right out of that front door, unlocking it and going to sit on the front porch swing in my nightgown. I would have no memory of doing this if my grandmother had not woken me up because the front door to her room was wide open and rain was blowing in. She went to close the front door only to find me sitting there on the front porch swing. She was startled at first to see someone there on the swing. As she came up to the porch and saw that it was me there, she called out to me, but I didn't respond. She was very worried because it was pouring rain outside, and while the front porch had a roof, the wind was blowing the rain onto the front porch. When I didn't respond to her call, she came closer to me and asked me what I was doing on the porch swing at this time of night. She said that I responded to her by saying, "I love the rain."

At this point she realized that something was not right and touched my arm. That's when I woke up to find myself sitting on the front porch swing in my long white nightgown with no shoes on. Because I was woken up, I vividly remember this night and still recall how it felt to wake up on the front porch swing in the rain. It's a very happy memory for me because I love the rain. Rain is very soothing to me, and I love nothing more than a rainy day! Getting to sit on a porch swing at night watching it rain would be something I would love to do. My parents have other memories of me sleep walking around the house around that age, but there were no other times when I went outside, thankfully.

Sleep walking is still being studied, with some research concentrating on sleep deprivation as somehow leading to sleep walking. While the person typically has no memory of sleep walking, they do still tend to remember their dreams. For example, when my grandmother woke me up on the front porch, I remembered that I was having a really great dream about being on a swing in the rain. I just didn't realize at the time how literal that experience was.

Sleep Talking

Sleep talking is something I have done several times. While my parents noticed that I sleep walked for a period of time, they also noticed that it stopped around the age of eleven. They had no idea that I talked in my sleep until two years later.

During this time, my family was preparing to move out of state, and all our furniture had already been packed up and taken by the movers. We were staying in a furnished apartment for a couple of weeks until we finished the school year and made the move. My father had gone ahead to where we were moving to handle things there while my mother took care of everything where we were living. Because of the tight quarters in the little apartment, I was sleeping in the same room as my mother, where there were two twin beds. The first night we moved in there, something very strange occurred, as my mother later told me and my grandmother.

There was a phone in the bedroom on the nightstand between the two beds so that my mother could receive calls from her work in the oil and gas business. She was leaving this job when we moved, and people were calling her to get information they needed before she was gone. In the past couple of months, she had been out in the field where the oil rigs were pumping and had collected a lot of data to report back about the status of the rigs and the production.

Late during the first night there, while I was sleeping she received a phone call from one of the engineers who had some detailed questions for her regarding the status of what was going on in one of the fields. The man on the phone was asking her questions, and my mother said that before she could answer him, I was answering the questions as if I had heard him on the phone.

That was strange enough, because this was before the age of cell phones. She was on a landline, holding the receiver of the phone to her ear, so it would be very difficult for me to overhear the conversation. Also, I was deep in sleep, which she could tell from my breathing, yet I continued to answer these questions that the man would ask before she could even respond to them.

Now here's the really interesting part: the questions were very detailed and specific to ratios and calculations regarding amounts of oil being retrieved and processed as well as timelines for certain parts of the project to be completed. No information of this kind was accessible to me, nor at that age did I pay much attention to what my mother did at work. Even if I had, these calculations and data were information that she had just received earlier that day, and she had not even had the time to look them over. That's why she wasn't responding quickly to each question, as each time the man asked her a question, she was looking through the reports in order to find the information.

To her great shock, each time she found the answer, I had already answered the question, and I was right every single time!

This continued for several minutes into the conversation, and at first she was fascinated hearing me give these replies. After a few minutes, though, the man could hear my voice in the background and asked who was there with her listening to the conversation. This was private, confidential information regarding this oil company and their oil wells, and he wanted to make sure no one was overhearing this sensitive data.

My mother replied that it was her daughter, and he said, "Okay, I'll wait. Get her back to bed before we go further." My mother knew she couldn't explain that I was asleep yet somehow talking in my sleep and giving correct answers to formulas and data before she could process it from the reports. So she put the phone down and woke me up.

I had no idea what was going on. She asked me if I could go into the living room and watch TV for a little bit as she was on the phone with work. I had no problem with this request, as it was a chance to watch late-night TV, which I wasn't often allowed to do.

When I went into the living room, I found my grandmother there watching a program and sat down next to her. She asked me what I was doing up at this late hour, and I explained to her that my mom was on a phone call. A little while later, my mother came into the room and told my grandmother and me what had happened.

"How did you know this information?" she asked me.

"All I remember is that you woke me up and asked me to come out here and watch TV."

She pulled out some of her research papers and asked me a few questions, and I laughed. "You expect me to know the answers to this? You know math is my worst subject. I have no idea how to do those calculations." I laughed at the incredulity of it.

When she told me and my grandmother what I had been doing, it was a shock to us all. As we discussed this anomaly, I shared that I had been dreaming about the oil field and that I would see the information in my dream about the oil rigs. Much like the dream in which I enjoyed being in the rain with my sleep walking, I had no idea that while I was dreaming about the oil fields, I was speaking this information out loud. In the dream, I was speaking with a man who wanted to know this information, and I was providing him with answers.

Learning to Sleep Talk in a Dream State

Edgar Cayce would lie in a dream state while conscious and lucid. He could quickly receive answers from almost any question spoken out loud to him. He was able to do this repeatedly yet unable to explain how the process occurred. It is still a mystery.

Cayce's method invites us to consider what outside stimuli enter our dreams while we are asleep. Can we absorb information like in the stories in which a person puts a book under their pillow? What if we sleep with the TV on—what type of information are we collecting from the news or other type of program?

Additionally, are we capable of sending telepathic information to each other as we dream? Was I telepathically reading the reports that my mother was holding while I was in a dream state? During the dream state, was I able to hear the questions coming from this man prior to him stating them out loud to my mother, so that I had the answers before she could even reply? Was it the act of my mother asking the questions out loud that triggered my response to answer out loud? Is this how it worked with Cayce—did he answer out loud because someone was there to ask him questions while he was in this state?

There are more questions than answers to types of experiences in which dreams interact with our psychic abilities. I don't know how to recreate sleep walking or sleep talking. I only have my personal experiences to share, and I hope they may be of some assistance to you if you have experienced these phenomena or know someone who has. In fact, I've tried to replicate my own Cayce type of experience while in a dream state. Here's how it began:

Replicating Cayce's Experience

The next person to notice my sleep talking was my husband. It began years later in a similar scenario with questions. He worked in IT, and when there's a problem in IT, everyone works around the clock to fix the problem until it's right.

He once received a call in the middle of the night about a technical problem. In this case, he had a cell phone and put the call on speaker so he could listen while typing on his laptop. He kept a desk in the bedroom for the late-night emergencies so that he could jump right out of bed and be on the computer when needed.

The problem he was dealing with had something to do with software, and they were asking him several questions about Unix and how things were operating on the servers. He was in deep thought, considering what the problem could be and where it stemmed from. While he was thinking about this, I spoke out loud in my sleep and began to give him information about Unix and where the problem was.

At first, he said that he responded to me, joking and saying, "Quiet down, woman. I'm working here." He thought that I was teasing him.

Instead of quieting down, I said, "The problem is with this," and gave him very technical information.

That time he listened and thought, *Could this be true?* He looked into it and discovered that was indeed the problem. He turned back to me and asked, "How did you know that?"

I didn't respond, as I was fast asleep. He shook me to wake me up. I asked what was wrong, and he looked at me confused.

"How did you know the answer to the problem?"

"What problem?"

It was then that he realized I had been sleep talking. He explained a little bit about what was going on at work and said he had no idea that I knew so much about Unix. I laughed and said that he knew full well that I didn't know anything about Unix. He then explained the depth and complexity of my answer to him and how it had led him to the solution. We were both surprised.

The next morning as we discussed what had happened with me further, he proposed that obviously somewhere deep in my brain I had the ability to understand very complex technical problems and that I could become a system administrator if I wanted to do so. My response was no way. I could never work on that stuff—it's too logic-minded and technical for me. I would be bored.

He asked if he could ask me other questions while I slept. We wanted to experiment and see what kind of things I knew about or had the ability to access from the akashic records, global consciousness, or other energy fields where I was obtaining this information. What was most fascinating to him was that when I was in this state, I didn't spend any time processing this information when it came through me. The answers were immediate and very specific.

We wondered if this was how it had worked for Edgar Cayce when he went into a light meditative state to receive the answers he did for his readings. Over time, as we experimented with my sleep talking, we found that I could answer questions about a wide variety of topics that I had no idea about when I was awake. Additionally, many times the answers related to topics that I not only had very little knowledge on but also tended to have very little interest in.

We also found that when I woke up, I would have been having a dream about the subject that I was being questioned on. I didn't like to do this exercise very often, as I felt that it disturbed my normal dream sequences as well as caused sleep deprivation from being woken up repeatedly throughout the night.

The one thing I would not do in this state was divulge any secrets. Some part of my consciousness was aware of the intention of the question and would not share information of a personal sort on anyone or about myself. The answers were typically more focused on information on large calculations, data retrieval, technical situations, and sometimes on future events.

This is all just another testament to how we are able to be psychic and pull information from the other planes, such as the global consciousness and many other levels, through dreamtime.

Nine

MANIFESTING YOUR DAYDREAMS

The concept of daydreaming is widely misunderstood. I believe that this confusion began when we were young. When we were caught not paying attention in school, our teacher would snap at us and tell us to stop daydreaming and focus. Because this was usually the only time adults mentioned daydreaming to us, we began to associate it with a bad behavior that would get us in trouble.

For most children, the only other time they are exposed to daydreaming as an activity is when they are watching cartoons. In the occasional cartoon, a character may be portrayed daydreaming, but it's typically a fantasy that is bizarre and out of this world. The character is quickly brought back to reality and forgets about the fantasy.

What if I told you that daydreaming is actually a powerful tool that can bring about positive changes and helpful answers to your daily life? For example, have you ever had one of those days when there is something you need to accomplish, but no matter how hard you try, it's just not working out? Maybe it's a deadline at work or a solution to a personal problem, and you just can't figure out what's best to do. Your thoughts about what would be the best solution are blank, and if you seek the advice of others, their opinions only serve to confuse you further.

As a writer, I've had days like this when the writing just won't come out of me. Outwardly, there's no difference in the day from yesterday when I was writing. I'm at the same desk, same computer, doing the same ritual to write, yet today it just won't come. Sure, I can type words, but the energy is not there. In that mode, I am not, as some would say, inspired. Others would describe this situation as having the dreaded writer's block.

In my early days, I used to try to force it. "I'm a professional writer," I would say to myself. "I'm smart and capable. I can figure out this problem. I just need to think harder so I can still write today. I'll force myself to stay here in this chair and write something. It will come."

Yet each time I did this, the answer to the problem was never the right one, and the writing that came out of me—well, let's just say it made its way to the delete pile the next day.

There's a reason why sometimes your mind has had enough and has put up a "Closed for Business" sign. Maybe it's overloaded and clogged with too much data. Maybe it's like a computer: it's running a backup of your mental hard drive and can't accept any more data at this time. Whatever the reason, you are not in the zone, where your best work comes from, and it's time to clear your mind.

When your mind is blocked, a mental refresh can allow us to get a new perspective on things. Daydreaming can be very helpful in this process.

Exercise: Using Daydreams to Open the Mind to New Ideas

Step 1: Clear Your Mind

It all begins with clearing your mind. The important bit to focus on is that it's time to walk away from the thought, the problem, the writing, or whatever it is that's not working for you at that time in order to relax. By doing so, you are giving your mind the time it needs to process other data that it's working on. You may be thinking, *How do I walk away from my thoughts? Won't my mind know that I'm leaving?* The next step will help with this mental adjustment.

Step 2: Leave the Room

To change your mind, the first thing to do is leave the room that you are in. According to a 2011 piece in *Scientific American*, there are studies detailing the "doorway effect," which states that when you pass through a doorway from one room to another, a psychological change occurs within you. These studies describe this as the reason people often forget what they were talking about or even why they left the room they were in after they walk through a doorway.

When you think about this, you'll realize you've done it before. You were thinking, *I need to go get this item, and it's in another room.* So you're walking through a room and thinking about things, perhaps even conversing with another person. Then you walk through a doorway, enter another room, and maybe again walk through another room, and all of a sudden you stand there in the room, looking confused, and think, *What did I come in here for?* You truly can't remember for a minute; sometimes it's even longer. You have forgotten why you came into the room and what you were looking for.

Many times you'll walk back through the first doorway, and after a minute or so, it's like a reset happens in your brain and you remember. *Of course*, you think, *I was going into the room to get that or to do this.* This time when you leave the room, you focus hard on what you are going to do. Many people will walk even faster from that room, with their head tucked down a bit as they quickly rush through the doorway and into the other room to retrieve the item. It's fascinating how our minds can be affected by a great variety of stimuli and can change instantly.

Once we walk out of the room where we were desperately trying to solve a problem or find an answer, we can take advantage of this doorway clearing, to leave that energy behind for a moment. We can then walk through another doorway and go outside for a breath of fresh air and take a quick walk or stretch our body to relieve the tension. We are clearing our mind in order to make room for new data and to think about the problem in a new way.

Step 3: Shake Your Body

This is where daydreaming can be most effective. Once you've left the room where you were working, it's time to find a comfortable spot in a different room or an area where you can sit quietly without interruption. Turn off your cell phone and find a private space where you won't be disturbed.

Now I want you to shake your body. Shake your shoulders, stretch your legs and arms, and shake them. Dance around and shake, and if you're not a dancer, just shake your body for a minute or two.

Yes, it might feel awkward to you if you're not a person who is used to dancing around, but shaking is an ancient practice that helps release physical tension and stress from the body.

Step 4: Relax

Once you've shaken your body, sit comfortably. Don't lie down, as you don't want to fall asleep and wake up hours later with everyone wondering where you've disappeared. Once you are seated, close your eyes and take three deep breaths in and out. Relax.

Step 5: Visualize

Create a picture in your mind of anything you find pleasant. A favorite place you love, a trip you've always wanted to take, a beautiful scene in nature, or a memory of time spent with someone you love or respect. Enjoy this journey. Take in the sights, sounds, and smells.

If you're doing this right, you'll notice that your body language has completely changed, and not only are you relaxed, but there's a big smile on your face that has occurred naturally. You are smiling while watching your dog run on the beach, riding the carousel in the park that you loved when you were young, or driving that convertible up in the mountains.

Whatever your pleasant memory or fun thought about something you wish you were doing, it should make you feel great. This is your daydream, after all. You don't even have to practice lucid dreaming—you know how to picture something in your mind and make it your own.

Step 6: Travel to a New Dream

Once you begin daydreaming, you may stay with this scene, or you may find that your thoughts drift and that as you grow tired of one scenario, a new thought pops into your mind. You think, *Oh yeah, I used to love doing that*, and in the blink of an eye, you've moved from being a young kid at the playground to the age you are now, dancing at a jazz club from the 1920s that doesn't even exist. You look amazing in your outfit, and everyone's dancing with you.

Step 7: Consider the Problem

After about five to ten minutes of playing in your daydreams, think about the problem you were facing earlier in the day. In this relaxed state of mind, ask your new, fun self what they would do with this problem. Allow yourself to see whatever fun and silly ideas your dreamy self wants to explore. The point is not that the exact answer will come to you but rather that the mind is relaxed and open to exploring all types of new ideas. Stay in this fun space for another ten minutes or so, having conversations with the people in your daydream and asking them what they would do to solve the problem. When you finish with your daydream, you may have received an inspired idea, or when you return to your work, inspiration may strike as you get back into the zone with renewed energy.

What Can Daydreams Do to Help?

In daydreams, something magical happens because you don't put any obstacles in your way. You can do anything with grace and ease.

In a rudimentary way, you are freeing your mind. It is not confined by the restrictive boundaries that you clog it with on a daily basis. Typically, when you have an irrational or illogical thought, you immediately dismiss it and admonish yourself for even having this thought. As an adult, you've become that teacher from your elementary school who told you to stop daydreaming and to pay attention. Now in your adult life, you are doing this self-limiting act to yourself with your thoughts and with your dreams.

Does this thought jar you? Are you realizing that you've been doing this to yourself, that you've been blocking your own creativity by creating these rigid walls around what you might perceive to be reasonable?

Good. I hope I've awakened you at this moment so that you'll begin to question and examine your thoughts and see how quickly you shut down anything that doesn't immediately sound reasonable to you. It's time to embrace what is truly possible and question the limiting beliefs that you've adopted over the years.

Do you know why some people are so creative and come up with the most imaginative ideas and inventions? It's because they think outside the box! The "box" is that wall that most people put up around their thoughts, shutting down any ideas that don't appear to be immediately logical, useful, and reasonable. People who have learned to ignore these self-limiting thoughts and run with the wild ideas that come to them understand that in order to create and find new solutions to problems, they cannot live with these boundaries.

If they're pretty good at this, they think outside the box.

If they're visionaries, they don't even have a box.

Take some time and think about this. Where do your thoughts go, and how are they boxed in?

Exercise: Taking Your Daydream to the Next Level

Let's revisit the daydreaming you used to find new ways of thinking, imagining yourself in all kinds of scenarios. It's time to take a break from what you're doing there in the dream and bring some focus into the picture.

Step 1: While still in your daydream, imagine yourself grabbing your favorite snack and finding a comfortable place to sit, on a bench, on a beach towel, in your mom's kitchen—anywhere that you feel safe and cozy in this dream.

Step 2: Now imagine a person that you greatly respect, whether it's a brilliant person from anywhere in the world or just someone who always gives you good advice. Picture them now here in this setting, in your daydream, and have a chat with them. Tell them about the problem you're working on and ask them what they think about it.

Step 3: You don't have to go into all the details. Because this is your dream, they already telepathically know about the problem. Relax and listen to what they have to say, and you may find that they give you the exact answer you need.

Step 4: When you come out of the daydream, it's time for action. Try out some of the ideas you had while daydreaming.

Here's an example: Let's say that someone is short on cash and is trying to find a way to make some extra money to supplement her income. In her daydream, she goes back to the home of her beloved great aunt who passed away several years ago. In this daydream, she's sitting at her aunt's kitchen table talking with her, explaining her cash-flow problem.

Her aunt is listening to her and begins to stir a bowl of batter, making something in her kitchen. As her aunt continues to busy herself in the kitchen, she begins to toss around ideas that her niece could try in order to generate new income while working from home. The daydreamer knows the solution is there if she can just put her finger on it.

As the daydreamer is thinking about this, her great aunt has left the kitchen and is now standing in the living room by her little writing desk. She loved that desk and would never let anyone touch it. In the daydream, she's looking at her niece as she's talking, and she keeps tapping on her writing desk, repeating her niece's words back to her.

"Yes," the aunt says while tapping on her desk. "If you could just put your finger on it."

When she comes out of the daydream, the daydreamer thinks about that writing desk and remembers that it's at her mother's house. She decides to go over and see her mom, and while she's there, she asks her mother if she can look at the writing desk. It struck her as important in the daydream, and she wants to have a look at that last fond memory of her great aunt.

Her mom says it's down in the basement, and as she heads down the stairs to its location, she get a little excited. It feels like a bit of an adventure.

She finds the writing desk and opens the drawers to peek inside. Inside the big drawer, she sees a stack of index cards tied together with a ribbon. She pulls out these cards and unties the ribbon to find all her great aunt's recipes. *She was such an amazing cook*, she thinks, and then it hits her: this is what she can do. She can use her aunt's recipes and start a business of her own on a very small scale by baking for family and friends. She asks her mom if she can have the recipe cards and shares her idea with her. Her mom, who has no interest in cooking, loves the idea and tells her that the recipes are all hers and to run with the idea.

In that moment, the creative ideas come pouring in. Her sister, who works long days at a corporate job and never has time to cook, would gladly hire her to prepare delicious, nutritious meals a couple of times a week that she could refrigerate and heat up for the family at night. Her cousin has three children and always needs baked goods to bring to after-school events and parties. Then there's her mom's best friend, who has been ill and has been trying to find a service to deliver meals, but she's only found a company who delivers from chain restaurants where the processed food is not agreeing with her or her dietary restrictions.

All of a sudden, she realizes that by a simple word of mouth to family and friends, she could be booked out and get this business off the ground with little cost and instant revenue. Not only has this solved her problem of how to quickly earn some extra money, it has the potential to create a business that she loves. And it all began with a daydream in which she was having a good time and visiting with someone that she loved.

Other Daydream Ideas
This is just one example of the power of daydreams and how they not only awaken your intuitive/creative mind but also es-

tablish the connection with your superconscious/higher self for inspiration and information.

If you don't want to imagine seeking another's advice for the solution to your problem in your daydream, place yourself in the comfortable setting I described earlier. Remind yourself that there are no wrong answers in your daydream and that there are hundreds of solutions to every situation. Imagine that you have no boundaries and have the power to do anything to this problem that you'd like. Maybe you picture that you are a superhero and have the power to dissolve the problem with your laser-beam eyes or to become invisible in this situation that you find distressing.

Daydreams Can Bring Clarity to Our True Desires

When we let go of the sometimes-confining boundaries of the logical mind and create a daydream scenario in which anything is possible, what usually comes out is the truth of what we really want to do were we given a no-holds-barred or no-boundaries permission to solve the problem. If you imagine you are a superhero with the power to dissolve the problem or become invisible, you may find that this is what you are wishing you could do to actually solve this problem. This may indicate to you that you need to make plans to leave this situation.

For example, perhaps you are at a job where you are truly unhappy. You've tried everything you know to be recognized and appreciated for your hard work, all to no avail. No matter how hard you try, your boss does not reward you for your work, and when he does notice you, he only seems to pile more work on you than on the others in the office, making you wish you could be invisible at times so that he wouldn't give you more to do. Your coworkers aren't bad to work with, but the company atmosphere has become so toxic that everyone is beat down and depressed, and all they know how to do is complain about what's gone wrong that day. Finding the energy every day to get up and go to work is taking more and more motivation, and you feel trapped and stuck in life.

Daydreaming that you are a superhero is your mind's and your soul's way of reminding you that you are stronger and more capable than you remember yourself to be. You have the power to change this situation by making plans to leave this job and to find new work where you will be recognized for your efforts and talents.

Sometimes we need to be reminded that it's okay to take our leave and go on to something new. We can become stuck when trying to fix a problem, thinking that it's too much trouble to put ourselves out there interviewing for a job and having to start all over again. While it does take effort to make that move, we soon realize that it was less stressful than what we were doing to ourselves working at a place that depleted our energy, destroying our hope and general satisfaction in life.

As the old saying goes, the only constant in life is change. Many times when we have a negative experience that we want to blame on others, it is actually the universe guiding us, prodding us, pushing us, and, at times, shoving us forward when it's time to have a new experience. That's the true power of daydreams. They can help us communicate with our higher consciousness and connect to our soul so that we can find a creative solution to our problem.

Let's return to our process of using daydreams to open the mind by walking through a doorway. You may find that when you walk back over that threshold, back through the doorway to your office, instead of pulling out your hair and stressing over how to get recognized for your efforts at work, you're taking the rest of the day off to update your résumé and look for a new place to work that excites you.

Or rather than spending the rest of the day stressed over how to make a bit of extra money, you've made three phone calls and have booked enough work through family and friends to make not only the money you needed for next week but also some extra to go do something fun.

That's just the beginning of what you can do with your daydreams. Inventors, entrepreneurs, visionaries, artists, writers, all creative types, and engineering types rely on the power of the daydream to assist them in their work. Now you know the secret of what daydreams can do for you. If you're ready, you can take it a step further and create an action plan for manifesting the daydream into reality by using the power of visualization.

Visualization Dreams

Visualization is the art of taking your creative idea and creating a roadmap of how you'll manifest this idea into being. The most important part of this process is to realize that you are creating a roadmap, but like all journeys, there are some detours, pit stops, and surprising adventures along the way.

Let's return to our example of the home baker who began looking for a simple way to make some extra money to supplement her income to pay her bills. Through her daydream, she was led to her great aunt's recipes and began baking goods for family and friends. Everyone is excited by the idea, and the money has started to come in. She is busy filling orders and doesn't have time to think about much else. She's loving this new creative journey and making more money than she originally needed. Deciding that she should indulge herself—after all, she's working so hard and making more money than she needed—she buys herself some things as a treat.

This continues for six months, maybe even for a few more, and she's getting comfortable with how things are going. She begins to rely on this income. She's even bought a new car, as she can easily afford the payments now with the extra money coming in.

Then one day, a few months later, it all starts to fall apart. First, her cousin calls: her husband has been offered a new job in Seattle, and they and their three kids are moving across the country in a month. There goes her baked-good orders for the after-school events. A couple of weeks later, her mother calls to tell her that her friend has really appreciated the meals she has provided for her, but she's decided to move in with her daughter, so it won't be necessary to continue with the meal service.

In the span of two months, she's lost two-thirds of her business, not by doing anything wrong, but simply through the ebb and flow of people and their needs. She still has the business from her sister, but even her orders have slowed down, as the kids are asking more often for their favorite pizza and takeout from restaurants for dinners.

Caught off guard, our daydreamer begins to lament about how the universe is against her and that everyone lets her down. What she really needs to think about is that while her business began with an inspired idea, the daydream is only the first step. Unless she also puts her daydream energy into creative visualization, it cannot grow and continue. In this state, it will dissipate, just like a dream. So our friend at this point has a tougher journey because she didn't understand how to take the second step and visualize where she wants her business to evolve and grow.

Let's help her get back on track. Here's what she needs to do:

Exercise: Manifest Your Daydream with a Vision Plan
Step 1: Create a Vision Plan
She needs to create a vision plan of where she sees her business going in the future. This can be drawn out on a big sheet of paper or in a notebook. In this vision plan, she draws a circle at the top to represent the business. From the circle she draws three lines that lead to three sections below the circle. She writes "Year One" at section one, "Year Three" at section two, and "Year Five" at section three, using a different color marker for each of these years.

Step 2: Reflect on Past Experience
Now it's time to brainstorm. She begins by writing on another sheet of paper, noting what went well on one side and what went wrong on the other.

On her went-well side, she writes that she discovered that she loves to bake, that her great aunt's recipes are amazing, and that people enjoy her personalized service. On the went-wrong section, she writes that she overestimated that business would continue in its current capacity forever and that she spent her earnings on herself rather than reinvesting in the business. She also was too scattered with what she baked and realizes it would be better to have weekly specials that served all her customers rather than bake unique items each week for each customer. Lastly, she realizes that she never gave any thought to expanding her customer base. Instead, she relied on her current customers to always be there, which is not sustainable or even practical.

Step 4: Daydream for Year One

Now that she has a better idea of what works and what doesn't, she can create her vision or visualization board. First, she goes back to what she's learned, beginning with letting go of the stress of the situation by daydreaming.

She finds a quiet space and shakes it off. Moving her body, she releases the fear and anxiety that has been building up in her. When we are stressed, we constrict our body and our mind, and it shuts down the flow of new energy and ideas, so it's important to do this mental reset first. She laughs as she shakes and dances and reminds herself that this all started with a dream and that the answers for what to do next will soon be clear to her. She then relaxes and prepares herself for a little time to daydream.

During her daydream, she reflects upon all the wonderful times that she has had with her business and notices the sweet memories of people who have enjoyed her cooking. She's resetting her mind and opening it to explore new ideas.

Step 5: Brainstorm

Emerging from her daydream, she has reset her thoughts, and her creative mind is back open and ready to work. She begins with brainstorming a one-year plan of what to do to grow the business.

Tapping into her daydreaming thoughts, she realizes that she already has the answer available to her from her current customers.

For example, she shouldn't have just relied on her cousin to place orders for after-school events almost every day. At all those sporting events, after-school events, and everything else her cousin's kids were involved with, she had missed a ripe opportunity to reach out to all of the other moms who were there at these events to offer them the same service. These moms had already sampled her baked goods and loved them. It wouldn't be a hard sell to get them to sign up for her baked goods like her cousin had, and she had one month before her cousin left town to drop in at all of these events and offer samples to all of the moms with her business card attached with instructions on how to place orders with her, including an offer for a 20 percent discount on their first order.

The same thought occurs with her mom's best friend. While she is now settling in at her daughter's home, she and her mother have plenty of friends who need this service and would greatly appreciate it. She takes her mom and her mom's friend out to lunch, and two hours later, both of them are on the phone acting as her new sales reps, recommending her services to all of their friends.

Two days later, she surprises her sister at her office at ten in the morning with a big basket full of goodies and a carafe of coffee and offers this midmorning pick-me-up treat to her sister's coworkers (after obtaining her permission, of course), giving her sister the first muffin. Attached to every baked good is the information on how to order baked goods from her for a variety of events. A week later, her sister calls to tell her that everyone loved her treats and that she wants to order two big trays of baked goods for a big meeting coming up next week.

Step 6: Note New Ideas

With just a few moves, letting go of the stress and fear and opening back up to her creative energy through daydreaming, she's completely changed the direction of her business for the next year. She has written these ideas in the section marked Year One on the vision board and put them into action so they may manifest into being.

Step 7: Daydream for Year Three

Feeling confident, she picks up a different-colored marker and begins to work on the three-year plan for the business. To visualize this, she'll need to practice daydreaming again. This time she'll need to imagine how far and how big she'd like the business to grow.

During this daydream, she'll run through the scenarios of seeing herself owning a bakery or a catering service and moving from baking in her home to a commercial kitchen or food truck. As she daydreams about this scenario, she'll experience pleasant sensations and see herself hanging a sign with the name of her new business outside the front window of the bakery, or—wait—it's just changed in her dream, and it's a café, where she also serves sandwiches, soups, and coffee to go with her baked goods.

In the blink of an eye, she's just seen where she wants to go with her business. Now she's ready to visualize on her board where she goes in three years. Looking over her list of what's worked and what hasn't, she realizes that this new goal means more to her than her original idea, which was just focused on how to make a little extra money to make ends meet. Now she is focused on pursuing her dream and seeing it come into fruition. She realizes that the extra money she was making and then spending on impulse items as quickly as she made it will now be funneled back into the creation of her new dream.

On her Year Three section of the vision board, she notes the profits being saved for the down payment and capital needed to open her own café. Because she's put the plan in writing on her visualization board, her goal has now moved from a daydream into a plan that she can visualize coming into being.

Step 8: Brainstorm and Daydream for Year Five

At this point, she can write out some ideas of what she might want to do by the fifth year. The ideas at this level are meant to be creative concepts and big dreams. She most likely won't know yet how to get to that level from where she is currently, and that's okay. Even if she tried to write a concrete plan, so many changes are going to happen along this journey that she may find that her business looks completely different from what she imagined it would be by year four. The point of visualizing year five at this point is to encourage her to dream big; if she could do anything she wanted, this is what she would create with her business.

In her year-five visualization, perhaps she dreams of having some of her baked goods discovered by a national company, and they buy her out and produce her baked goods using her great aunt's recipes, which have been enhanced by some flavors of her own along the way. Or maybe she dreams of having built a franchise of cafés that began with six stores in her state and is now looking at going national. She may dream that she expands her brand in the grand style of Martha Stewart, where she incorporates entertaining and decorating and builds an empire of her own. Year five is meant to hold these types of dreams, which, given the chance, you could take as far as they can go and as far as you would love to see them go.

This is the power of creative visualization and manifestation. It begins with a daydream, and then, by taking action and creating a plan, you can visualize your daydream into being. The dream becomes your reality.

While I used an example of a woman with a baked goods business, the steps shared here can apply to anything in your life that you would like to create. This exercise works for everyone, no matter what your plan looks like.

If only teachers understood the creative potential of giving students ten minutes to daydream after finishing the day's lessons—it could change our world.

Conclusion

BELIEVING IN THE POWER OF YOUR DREAMS

It's been my distinct pleasure to be of service to you as your travel guide to the other side. Through this book and the other books in my Awakened series, I have invited you to awaken to your higher self and to explore the magic of who you truly are. I hope that on this particular journey you have enjoyed exploring the power of your dreams.

Whether it has helped you understand your dreams better, helped you grow empowered through your dream states, or encouraged you to take hold of your daydreams to manifest a life that you once thought impossible, my wish for you is that the best and brightest of your dreams come true.

As part of our destiny here on earth, we as a group evolve on a continual basis. This is never more apparent or more stressful than it is during a new age. This major energetic shift is occurring within each of us at this time, and as with any change, there is resistance, which can cause the darkest of times as people react in fear. During these times, it can be easy to forget how amazing we as humans really are and how much good there is in the world.

Many people are having dreams that tell what the future will be like for us all. Some see the tough times to come, while others see the promise of what things will look like once we settle in to this new energy. Using the power of your dreams, perhaps now you will see what the future holds for you.

In my work as a teacher and coach, I share that we are creators with our thoughts, and as such, the future outcome of what we desire and dream about manifesting can literally occur in months, weeks, or sometimes even days. The important thing to remember is how powerful you truly are as a dreamer and as a conscious creator. This magical power begins with believing in the power of your dreams and then taking the necessary actions to bring them into this earthly world.

Being dreamers and conscious creators is one of our greatest gifts; however, whether or not we choose to take action on these dreams is all up to our free will. No matter how wonderful our dreams are, the future depends on the actions we take to further our hopes, dreams, and ideas.

Now you know the secrets of how powerful your dreams and daydreams can be. Seize the day and the night—your future is waiting for you now in your dreams.

Appendix

COMMON DREAM SYMBOLS

In this book, we've discussed what some dream symbols mean, including flying, falling, losing your teeth, and being chased. I discussed these four in greater depth because they are some of the most common dreams that a majority of people have sometime in their lifetime.

I've also explained that while you can look at symbols and see what they could mean, they should not be used as the only guide to interpret your dream. In an earlier chapter when I shared the dreams of clients who dreamt of powerful symbols, such as a wolf, we could see that we had to take in all the aspects of the dream to really understand what the wolf meant and why it changed over time into a sweet puppy.

I'm including this appendix in the book with some definitions of symbols and potential meanings, but remember, the best interpreter of your dreams is always you. You know better than anyone else what is going on in your life and can look at these symbols in regard to what you are dealing with in your daily life to discern what they symbolize.

I'm listing some of the most popular dream symbols here in this chapter, but I recommend that you check out some dream books that are large encyclopedias that list thousands of dreams symbols and what they can mean. It's always good to have one of these dreams books in your library as a ready reference guide.

If you have a dream that is particularly memorable to you or if it recurs, you may find that a dream interpreter can help-explain the meaning of the dream. In the old days, every village had an oracle, a dream interpreter, a wise woman, or a shaman who assisted in interpreting dreams. It was helpful to have someone in your local area who could interpret your dreams, as they understood the local cultural and societal mores and practices of the area.

This is one of the reasons that the symbols cannot be the end-all, absolute meaning. One culture can see a raven as a harbinger of good news, while another culture sees it as an omen of terrible things to come. So your dreams are partly affected by your spiritual and cultural beliefs.

Take this into account when you are looking at symbols and what they mean to you.

Alligator

In many dreams, an alligator represents something hidden that has yet to rise to the surface. It means to pay attention to the danger that lurks nearby.

For many people, this is the meaning of an alligator, yet I happen to adore alligators. They bring back good memories of my hometown in Louisiana. When I dream about an alligator, it's always a good dream for me, and it is typically a message from my father, who often appears as an alligator in my dreams. Keep in mind that no matter the typical meaning of a symbol, it may have very different personal significance to you.

Alligators are a symbol of masculine energy. My alligator dreams are always friendly and fun. I love alligators, have them in decor in my home, and even wear jewelry with them. Even the symbol of something emerging that was hidden by the alligator can be a sign of something good coming. You may encounter a surprising incident that could be startling at first, but the opportunity is there for growth and evolution from the experience.

Angel

Dreams with angels are usually visitation dreams in which you are truly being visited by an angelic being from the other side. If it is truly a visitation, you will see the brilliant light around the angel and will feel very positive energy emanating from this being. If you don't feel this incredible positive energy, it is something else masquerading as an angel, and you should send it away.

A visit from an angelic being is a blessing. They come as messengers to show that you are loved and under their protection. Pay special attention to anything that the angels are holding in their hands, as these will be symbols of the gifts they are bringing to you.

Apple

Eating an apple in a dream means that you are open to gaining wisdom through your actions. It is a symbol of the goddess or divine feminine energy, as seen in the five-pointed star created

by cutting the apple in half. It can also indicate you are opening to your intuitive side.

Apples have been misrepresented in many stories as being a temptation. Pay attention to what you do with the apple
in your dream or how the apple is being used in the dream.
Are you eating the apple while looking into someone's eyes?
This indicates you are awakening your knowledge, whether
that be carnal knowledge or esoteric wisdom. If the apples are
bright and shiny in a bowl, it means that the information being shared with you in the dream is very helpful and good. If
the apples are turning brown or looking rotten, it means the
opposite, that the information someone is sharing with you in
the dream is not helpful and you should not trust what this
person is telling you.

Baby

Many people think that when they dream that they are pregnant, this means they are going to become pregnant, but this
is generally not the case. (See the entry for pregnancy.) When
there is a very good chance that you or someone in your life
is about to become pregnant, it is more likely that you will
dream about a baby.

Many times, the it's the soul of the baby, introducing themselves to you from the spirit world. You may hold the baby in
your dream as you get to know them. A crying baby indicates
that there is some emotional tension around the relationship
between you and your partner. A laughing baby indicates that
the couple is very happy together and that the baby will be an
added blessing to the family.

Beach

In brief, water symbolizes the emotional field, and land or the beach symbolizes the mental field. To understand more about what the ocean means in your dream, see the entry for water. The beach represents the portal, the connection between the mental field and the emotional field.

Notice how you feel in this dream on the beach. Are you looking out at the shore and enjoying the feel of the sun and the sound of the waves? Do you feel like you are on vacation? Are there palm trees swaying in the breeze? Dreaming about the beach could be from the conscious mind if you are about to go on vacation, but if it's just in a random dream, you are about to have an awakening. Your emotions and your thoughts are bringing you to a new understanding about a situation in your life and possibly a new beginning. This is usually a deep, introspective revelation of some kind.

If you dream that you are walking on the beach, where are you walking? Are you walking toward the water, to connect with your emotional side, or away from the water, to go contemplate the situation, or are you walking along the beach, which indicates balancing your thoughts and emotions?

Bird

Consult a dream dictionary to get specifics on the type of bird in your dream, because each bird carries a special message of its own. In short, when you dream of a bird, it means a message will soon be delivered to you.

If the bird is in a nest, you may be looking for a new home soon. If you dream of a nest full of eggs, it can indicate money coming your way. If the bird is singing or flying, it means that a wish is coming true for you. If birds are attacking you, you have taken on too many obligations and cannot handle all the responsibilities given to you. If you dream of a dead or dying bird, you are experiencing a great disappointment in a hope or dream that you are now realizing won't come to fruition.

Boat

After dreams of being on a boat, begin by referencing the meaning of water in a dream to determine your emotional state. Next, notice the size of the boat. If you are on a cruise ship, you are along for the ride with many other people and don't have to give much thought or energy to where you are going in life at the moment. If you are alone in a small boat, like a canoe or rowboat, it implies that you will have to do the work yourself and that it will require some effort and action on your part, like rowing the boat. If you are on a sailboat and heading out into the ocean, you are embarking on a new journey or starting something new. If you are the captain of the ship, it's a very positive sign that you have everything you need to make a wish or dream come true; you just need to set sail and have faith that you can do this. A kayak represents someone who is working to have balance between the mind, body, and spirit.

Book

If you are reading a book and the last page says "The End," you are closing a chapter of your life and walking away from your life as you've known it. If there is a stack of books on your desk, it indicates that you are prepared and knowledgeable for the task at hand. If you dream of being in a library, it means that you will be given great knowledge about a topic or subject that you are interested in, but it will take time and you must be patient and willing to go the distance to receive this information.

Bridge

Dreaming about a bridge is similar to dreaming about the beach. The bridge is another portal, something you cross over to get from one phase in your life to another or from one state of mind to another. If you are happy to cross the bridge, you are open-minded and ready to receive new information and experiences. If the bridge is blocked, broken, or in disrepair, you have severed the connection between one part of you and another, such as staying too deeply in your thoughts and the worries of your logical mind while blocking off all of your emotions and intuition that can help give you a sense of what is going on.

If you are standing on the bridge but are afraid to walk forward or drive over it, you are struggling with issues of self-esteem and self-confidence. You do not feel that you are strong enough or good enough to move forward. If you dream that you fall off the bridge, you are dealing with subconscious fears of failure.

If you jump from the bridge, your fears are giving you the impulse to run away rather than to face your fears head on. Jumping from a bridge usually indicates that the fears are not real but rather in your overactive thoughts and worries. The size of the bridge indicates how big your fears are, and the height can indicate how far you have to travel to reach this new destination. If someone is waiting for you at the other end of the bridge and waving you on, you have others who are willing to support you in this new journey.

If you are driving over the bridge, the color of the car also indicates your emotional state. Lights on the bridge indicate moments of inspiration and clarity. Fog on the bridge indicates that the state of your mind is clouded with too many concerns.

Butterfly

Butterflies are very often visitations in dreams, as they represent the soul of a loved one who has come to visit. They can choose to come as a butterfly, as it is easier for someone who is grieving the loss of a loved one to see them in this form than their human form. Many times it means to pay attention when you are out in the world, and when you see a butterfly, it is this loved one announcing their presence to you and that they love you and are watching over you.

Butterflies indicate transformation from one form to another, from the caterpillar to the butterfly, from the person in their physical body to the soul in the spirit world. In many dreams, the butterfly can indicate that you will undergo a metamorphosis in which you are about to experience great change and have a personal transformation. Many times this is a spiritual awakening, but it can be for any aspect of your life.

Cat

A dream about a cat can mean a variety of things. If it's a particular breed, consult a dream encyclopedia. The first thing to consider is how you personally feel about cats. Are you a cat person, or do you not care for them? What is the cat doing in the dream? Is it purring and content or screeching and on the prowl? This can be interpreted similarly for any member of the cat family, including tigers, leopards, panthers, mountain lions, and cougars. If the cat is menacing toward you in the dream, it can mean that a negative experience will pop up out of nowhere soon. Think of how a cat in the wild can remain hidden until it pounces.

If you like cats and the cat is playful and friendly in your dream, it means that you are being perceived as strong and independent. If the cat just looks at you in the dream or gazes at you and then sits nearby licking its paw, it indicates that magical abilities are coming to you.

Celebrity

Many people dream about a favorite celebrity in a dream. Often they are out somewhere with them or making love to them. In these dreams, it's not that they want to be with that celebrity but rather that they wish to possess the personality, charisma, charm, gifts, or talents that this celebrity displays.

Men often dream about comic book characters that are hero archetypes to them. Yes, fictional characters are celebrities in their own way. Women often dream about their ideal romantic dream-man celebrity, wishing that they would be romanced like the love interest of this celebrity in a movie role. When you dream of a strong, powerful celebrity who takes charge, saves the world, gets rich, pulls one over on the bad guy, and so on in a movie, you are looking to find this power within yourself. If you dream that you are a celebrity, walking the red carpet or with photographers surrounding you, it means that you are looking for affirmation and acknowledgment from others that you are special and are doing a good job in whatever you are doing or creating.

Champagne

Champagne is more common in dreams than any other alcoholic beverage, more so than wine, beer, or mixed drinks. Whether or not you like the taste of champagne, it appears often in dreams because we associate champagne with toasting to the good life, a great success, a wedding, or the start of something new and wonderful. Toasting with champagne means that your higher self is already celebrating the fortuitous news and awards and recognition to come. Enjoy—good news is on the way. In the dream, notice if you are celebrating alone, with a special person, or with a group of people. This will give hints to what the celebration is related to, be it work, family, your love life, or a personal achievement. If the champagne is flowing like a fountain and lots of people are celebrating, some fabulous news is on the way!

Cheating

Dreams about someone cheating on a partner are very common. Sometimes they are literal, an intuitive sign that you are being cheated on. If that's truly the case, you won't just dream about it—you will feel it intuitively when you're awake, and signs will keep popping out around you.

Most times, though, cheating dreams have to do with insecurity and feeling that you are not good enough for your partner, so it's just a matter of time before they realize this and leave you for another person. When you dream of this scenario, it's time to work on yourself and to practice some self-love and encouragement. Make a list of all the wonderful things that you bring to the relationship.

If self-confidence is not your problem, then a dream of cheating implies that you don't fully trust the person in the dream who is cheating on you, whether or not they are being sexual with another person. They could be an untrustworthy person by lying to you about who they are, what they do, or what goes on in their life and career. They could be stealing from you, doing things behind your back, and setting you up to get taken advantage of.

If the dream is about you cheating on your partner, it implies that you are not feeling satisfied in the relationship and that you are looking outward to feel acknowledged and understood. In a sense, you feel that you are being cheated out of something in the relationship, not given enough time together, not getting enough attention, or not being satisfied in some way. This is a warning sign that it's time to connect and share your feelings with your partner so that you can work together to bring intimacy on the mind-body-spirit level in order for the relationship to evolve and for the two of you to grow closer and more intimate.

Church

If you dream about an Old-World type of church with a steeple, it indicates a message is being delivered to you from the higher planes of the spirit world. If you are in a church that you do not recognize and the people are not kind to you, it implies that you are feeling unfairly judged by others who have no reason to be judging you. If you walk into a dark church with no one inside, it can mean you will be attending someone's funeral in the near future. If you are in a church where the choir is singing, good news will be revealed to you soon. If you dream that you are always late to church, you are not giving the needed attention to your spiritual self.

If you are in an old European church or cathedral in your dream, it means you will connect soon with a past-life memory. If there are gargoyles on this old church, the number of gargoyles indicates the number of people or guides who will help you reconnect with this past-life memory.

Clothing

When you notice what you are wearing in a dream, the color of the clothing is most important. Consult a dream dictionary about what colors mean or consult my book *The Awakened Aura* to see what each color means on a mind-body-spirit level.

The size and state of the clothing is also very important. If you dream of being formally dressed in a tuxedo or ball gown, you are wishing to be seen in a romantic way or in high esteem for who you are. If your clothes are tattered, dirty, and worn, it indicates how you are feeling about the state of your life at the moment and how worn out you are by your life. If your clothes are too baggy, you are feeling self-conscious about showing the world who you truly are. If the clothes are too tight, too overtly sexy, or way too loose and baggy, you are struggling with your feelings of how you are perceived in your physical body and how attractive you are to others. Dreaming that you are in a wedding dress pretty obviously indicates what you are wishing for.

If your clothing is torn off of you in a dream, you are worried about a secret you are hiding being exposed. If you drop part of your clothing, such as a scarf, hat, glove, or handkerchief, you are secretly wanting to be exposed and to have your secret come out into the open.

If you are dressed inappropriately in your dream in comparison to the event, such as old gym shorts when everyone else is in formal wear, it indicates that you are unsure of your status in life and whether you can trust the people in your life. It can also indicate that your friends are not giving you the best advice.

Dancing

To dance in a dream is typically a good thing. It means that you are in the flow, engaged in the rhythm of your life, and making your way through it. The style of dancing indicates the progress you are making and how you are most comfortable in your life. If you are line dancing to country music, you like a sense of order and being part of a team. If you are dancing in a gown at a ball, you appreciate the finer things in life and want to live a more glamorous life. If you are slow dancing with someone you love or are attracted to, you are wanting to get closer and more intimate with this person. If you are at a party dancing with friends, you are opening up to being more social in the future. If you are at an event and are happily dancing by yourself, you are experiencing a breakthrough in which you and your sense of self-worth will shine for all to see.

Demon

In most dreams, seeing a demon or dark figure represents the shadow side of yourself. It's a dark aspect of your personality that you prefer remain hidden, and you do not like to think about it. It's showing itself because you are struggling with your thoughts and feelings about something that is upsetting or worrying you.

On a few rare occasions, it could be something from a lower spiritual plane that has entered your dream, in contrast to a visitation from an angel that is from the higher spiritual planes. You will sense that difference because of the feeling of cold, dreadful energy, unlike the warm, loving energy of the angel. If you sense this energy in your dream, banish it immediately, put up your white-light shield, and state that this being can never return.

If you dream about another person you know turning into a demon, it indicates that they are struggling with their shadow side and that they are heading into trouble on the wrong path. Most likely at this point they are not open to interference by you and will not take your offer of help well.

Dog

In most cases, to dream of a dog is a happy thing. Dogs represent loyalty, fidelity, and friendship. Men tend to have more dreams of dogs than women do. If you dream of a pack of dogs, it's a sign that it's time to make new friends and grow closer to them. If the dog is happy and playful, you are in a good situation in your life. If the dog is anxious and barking, you are being warned that someone who doesn't mean well is coming your way and to be ready. There are so many breeds of dogs, and the type of dog that you dream about gives many clues to the dream, so consult a dream dictionary that describes the meaning of the breed of dog.

Dolphin

To dream of a dolphin means that someone from the other planes is trying to establish telepathic communication with you. You may have noticed high-pitched sounds lately. These are also indications of someone in spirit attempting to speak to you. The dolphin is asking you to take a moment to relax and pull away from your work and everything that is keeping you busy. In order to receive a message from spirit, you have to be in a relaxed state to hear what they are trying to communicate. Take a break, go do something fun, and then relax, open up, and ask to receive the message.

Eyeglasses

To dream of wearing eyeglasses to see in the distance indicates that you are uncomfortable with seeing what the future holds. If you are wearing glasses to see things up close, this means that you are not wanting to clearly see what is going on around you in your daily life. If you willingly wear the glasses and look around, you are opening up to understanding what has really been going on around you that you have been resistant to seeing. If other people are wearing glasses and you aren't, they are scrutinizing you and your work and are going to start pointing out some errors that you are making.

Fire

To dream about a nice fire that you are kindling and enjoying means that you are open to socializing and caring for others. If you dream about a fire that is large but not out of control and is all around you, you are being purified and transformed like the phoenix. In these types of purification dreams, you are aware of the fire, but it is not hot; it is cool and does not harm you.

With fires that are raging out of control and burning something down, such as a home or building, pay attention to what and where the fire is burning, as it will give clues to what is being destroyed and why. Trying to put out the raging fire can indicate that you are feeling stressed and overwhelmed in your life, like you are always on call, trying to put out fires. If in a dream you see someone you know set fire to something that you love, this person is envious of you. If you are setting fire to something of yours, you are feeling backed into a corner and that you have no other alternatives but to cut your losses and run.

Flirting

Dreams about flirting are slightly different from dreams about cheating. In cheating dreams, there is an issue of trust present. In flirting dreams, you are experiencing the desire for an emotional connection with your partner, or if you're single, with someone new. It indicates that you are open and ready to experience affection. If you are dreaming that you are flirting with someone other than your romantic partner, it indicates that you are not feeling that intimacy is strong in your relationship. If you dream that your partner is flirting with someone else, it means that the connection between the two of you is growing apart. It's time to have a talk with your partner and both commit to making a conscious effort to reconnect on the mind-body-spirit level in your relationship.

Forest

If you dream of being lost in a forest or jungle but are calm and making your way through, it indicates that you have good instincts and self-confidence. When faced with a new challenge, you handle it well. It also means that a new opportunity is heading your way if you're willing to seek it out.

If you're trapped in the jungle or forest and are feeling scared, it means that you are feeling overwhelmed by a situation in your life. The other symbols in a forest or jungle dream will give clues to the new opportunity or the situation in which you are feeling overwhelmed, whether it's in your personal life or career. If you find your way out of the forest before you wake up from this dream, you are close to figuring out the problem in your life and solving it. If you wake up from the dream feeling scared and still stuck in the jungle, you are feeling like you don't know a way out of your current problem.

Funeral

Dreams about funerals can sometimes be prophetic dreams. Abraham Lincoln's dream about attending his own funeral is probably the most famous of this type. Like all dreams, pay attention to how you feel in the dream and how real the dream feels. If this dream recurs, it can indicate a prophetic dream of something to come.

Most dreams of a funeral, though, indicate putting something to rest, letting something go, or ending a period in your life. Pay attention to what is being buried: Is it someone you know, indicating a change in your relationship with that person? Or is it a different type of item that the funeral is being held for? This item will symbolize what is ending in your life.

Garbage

If you dream that you are picking things up and throwing them into the garbage or that you are taking the garbage out, it means you are letting go of the clutter in your life, whether it's physical items that are holding you back or emotional and mental baggage that is weighing you down. The bigger the bag of garbage, the more you are letting go. If you dream that you are surrounded by garbage or are in a garbage dump, it is the opposite: your mental, emotional, and even physical problems are piling up and weighing you down.

Ghosts

The most famous ghost dream story might be *A Christmas Carol*, in which Scrooge is visited by the ghosts of Christmas Past, Present, and Future in order to learn about his future. In my world, we refer to this incident as a prophetic dream. I put ghost in this common list of symbols not because people often dream about ghosts, but to bring to your attention that you may be visited by one while sleeping. Many people discount this ghostly visitation as a dream because it is easier to deal with than the surprise of having seen a ghost.

The most common dream about a ghost, however, involves a haunted house. You are scared and sense the house is haunted by a ghost. The easiest way to determine if a ghost is actually visiting you or if the dream is about a ghost is that if you are living in a haunted place, you'll see this ghost again. If you are sleeping in a haunted hotel, you may only experience the ghost once, but it will enter your dreams in a random manner. You won't be dreaming about anything scary or haunted; rather, your dream will draw you into a personal story the ghost is trying to tell you.

Hair

Hair is a very powerful indication of how we are feeling in our dreams. If you dream about your hair and it is long and beautiful, you are connected to your power and sensuality. If your hair is flowing in the wind, you are usually happy and enjoying life. If your hair is piled up or pulled back into a bun and you pull out the pins or hair band to let your hair cascade down, you are literally letting your hair down to have some fun and are not going to be as stressed and uptight about the situation that you are dreaming about. If you dream that you are cutting your hair short or getting your hair cut short, you are about to change your life in a big way. This dream will often follow a real visit to the hairdresser to get a major hairstyle change.

If your hair is not super dark but you dream about dying it black, it means that you are not ready to reveal your inner secrets and want to keep them hidden for a while longer. If you dye your hair blonde in a dream and you are not a blonde in life, it means that you are looking to lighten up about things in life and not take whatever you are dreaming about too seriously. If you dream that you are dying your hair red, you are looking to awaken your passion and creativity and explore something new.

If your hair falls out in a dream or you dream that you are going bald, this indicates that you are feeling vulnerable about the changes in your life and fear that there is nothing that you can do about them. If you dream that you are stroking someone's hair and that person is not your current love interest, it indicates that you are having feelings for this person and want to pursue a relationship with them. If you are stroking a loved one's hair, including family members and children, it indicates your deep love and care for them.

Hallway

Hallway dreams are similar to bridge dreams but not as dramatic. They are the early beginnings to a new venture, to exploring something new. If all the doors in the hallway are closed, you are preparing to make a new decision and don't have all of the information you wish you did. If you try to open a door and it is locked, this particular opportunity is not going to present itself to you. If all the doors are locked, new opportunities are not going to present themselves to you at this time, even as you are looking for a way out.

If you choose one of the doors, open it, and walk into a new room, notice who is in this room and what else is in the room. The people will give clues to who will be helping you with this new opportunity, and the items in the room indicate what the opportunity is about.

In hallway dreams, most people typically don't dream about reaching the end of the hallway. Sometimes another figure or person will appear at the end of the hallway to deliver a message, or a person who is visiting from the spirit world will walk down the end of the hallway to return to the spirit world.

Hotel

In dreams in which you are in a hotel, it's all about the symbolism of the hotel where you are staying. Is the hotel luxurious, plain, a bed-and-breakfast, or a run-down, scary place? The condition of the hotel shows your feelings about the condition of things in your life. What floor are you staying on? The higher the floor, the better things are going in your life. What does your room look like? Are you surrounded by a comfortable, beautiful, and relaxing space, or is it sparsely decorated and dirty? Everything in the hotel is a hint to what's going on in your life—how the bellman treats you, what the check-in service is like, and so on. Pay attention to it all, as it's giving you a report card of how things are going in your world.

Because the dream is in a hotel, it indicates that this is a temporary situation and is giving clues about what is about to change in your life in the near future.

House

House dreams are similar to hotel dreams in that you need to pay attention to every detail in the home, the condition that it is in, where you live and sleep, how you feel in the rooms, and how others treat you in the dream. To dream about your home indicates what is going on in your life, and it's not about to change unless you take action to change it.

If you dream about your childhood home and that's a happy memory, some good news is coming your way for you or your family. If you dream about a happy experience in your current home, you are in a good place in life and feeling satisfied. If you dream about your current home and it is strangely in very bad condition, it could be a warning of an illness to come for someone living in the home. If the dream is about a home being torn down or falling down, it indicates that someone in the home is looking to break up the family unit and go their separate way.

Insect

Dreaming about insects and bugs is pretty literal and similar to what it means when you see them in person. They are irritating and imply that something is bugging you. They are pests, and someone or something in your life is becoming a pesky problem that will continue to bother you until you deal with it. Consult a dream encyclopedia to find out more about the particular type of pest.

Internet

When you dream that you are logging on to the Internet, it typically means that you are ready to explore and learn new things and that you are ready to approach life on a grander scale and meet new people. Many times it means that you will travel soon, meet new people, or take a course to learn something new.

Jail

Most dreams about being imprisoned, behind bars, or in jail are about feeling restricted in life. They are usually associated with guilt of some kind, feeling that you did something wrong or that you are trapped in a job you don't like, in a relationship that isn't working, or in some aspect of your life that isn't going well. Notice how you feel in the cell. Are you wishing for freedom, or do you just feel stuck? Do you feel for some reason that you deserve to be there, or do you feel like someone else is responsible for you being there and that they should be in jail instead?

Jewel/Jewelry

It's rare for a dream about jewels or jewelry to be a bad thing, unless you dream about your jewels being stolen by thieves. To dream of receiving jewels or wearing jewelry represents your personal value and how the outside world perceives you. Thus, the larger the jewels, the more renowned you are.

The type of jewel and type of jewelry indicate your growth and evolution. Wearing a crown or tiara indicates spiritual gifts and growth coming to you. Wearing a ring indicates love coming your way. A long necklace symbolizes a very long, good-standing reputation in the community and being seen as successful and trustworthy by others. A short necklace, like a choker, represents the fifth chakra and suggests that your powers of communication and suggestions in presentations will be well received.

The color of the jewel is very important, as the colors correspond to the chakras. For example, ruby red is the first chakra and represents stability and being grounded. Green is the heart chakra and indicates love; if it is a sickly lime green, it indicates the heart turning from love to jealousy. Blue is communication, gold is action and masculine energy, and silver is receiving and feminine energy. If you are wearing a bracelet in your dream, notice which wrist the bracelet is on. Worn on the left wrist, it indicates gifts coming to you from another; worn on the right wrist, it indicates rewards coming to you from your hard work.

Pearls imply wisdom, and the person wearing them is generous and full of integrity. They also indicate that prosperity and good luck are on the way.

Jungle

See Forest.

King

If you are a woman and you dream about a king, that person represents the masculine person that you see as an authority in your life. If this man is kind and loving in the dream, you have chosen a good partner. If this king is cruel and overbearing and forceful, you are being warned that you are in a position with this person in which you will not be treated well or fairly.

If you are a man and you dream about being a king, it indicates that you are about to come into a position of strength, power, and authority. If the dream is celebratory and people are happy to see you as the king, it indicates that this new transition will be well received. If you have to fight someone in order to become king, pay attention to the person you are fighting and the symbols around them, as this will give you clues as to who your adversary is in real life.

Kissing

If you dream that someone kisses your hand, it means they are reaching out to you in respect. If you kiss someone you know and like in a dream, it indicates your fondness for them. If someone grabs you and kisses you against your will in a dream, they mean you harm in one way or another, and you should not trust this person.

Lollipop

There are lots of dreams about candy. Consult a dream encyclopedia about the meaning of the different types of candy to delve deeper. However if you dream that you are licking a lollipop in a dream, it indicates that you are opening up to your sensual side and are ready to explore new things sexually.

Lottery

Typically, to dream that you have won the lottery—sadly, I'm here to report—doesn't mean that you are about to win the lottery. It can in a few prophetic instances, but typically not. If you dream about numbers to play in the lottery, that's a better indication that you may be closer to winning the lottery. Dreaming about winning the lottery indicates your desire to have something come quickly with little effort on your part to solve your problems. You want fast relief without having to do much to get there. It also means that if you choose a fast and seemingly easy solution to the problems you are experiencing in the dream, the problems won't be resolved. They will just lead to more problems that eventually will grow so large that you will be forced to take action and take care of them.

Mail

To dream about receiving a letter in the mail indicates that a person from your past, particularly an older person, will be contacting you soon. To dream about emails piling up in your inbox indicates the frustration you are feeling about having too much to do.

Mansion

A mansion dream is similar to a house dream, with the exception that if you are moving into the mansion, it indicates that you are moving up in life—in health, wealth, or social status. If you are being thrown out of a mansion at a party, it indicates that you are about to experience an embarrassing social and public situation. As in house dreams, pay attention to the style, decor, and people at the mansion.

Mermaid

If you dream that you are a mermaid, you are opening to your divine feminine power. You are ready to feel free, independent, and in control of your life. You are a sensual person and do not like being contained, confined, defined, or controlled by others.

If you dream that a mermaid visits you, she is inviting you to open up to these aspects of yourself. If the mermaid is under the moonlight, she is inviting you to open up to your psychic abilities. If she is combing her hair and gives the comb to you, it is a very rare and special gift, giving you control over your emotions and the ability to weather all types of storms in your life.

Money

To receive a large sum of money in a dream indicates that wealth of some kind is coming to you soon. The most important thing to pay attention to in this dream is how the money came to you. Consider who gave you the money and then what you did when you received the money. If you dream that you are losing money, it indicates where your thoughts and worries are about your current finances and cash flow.

Mountain

If you are climbing a mountain in your dream, it indicates that you are making steady and sure progress in achieving your goals. If you are coming down the mountain, it means that this goal is not what you thought it would be and that you have decided to abandon this journey and will set out to try something new. If you are somewhere looking at the mountains, it indicates that you are opening up to looking at new dreams. If you dream you are falling off a mountain, it means that you do not have the resources available to you at this time to reach the success that you are working toward, so you will need to reach out for reinforcements.

Nurse

Men dream more about nurses than women do. When a man dreams about a nurse, it typically does not mean he has an illness. Rather, he has an emotional need for someone to love and care for him. He is opening up to being loved and showing affection. If the dream is one-sided, though, and the nurse comes and cares for him but he does not engage with her otherwise, it indicates that he is struggling with being selfish and not giving of himself in relationships. Women dream more often about a nurse giving a message about the status of a situation.

If a nurse walks out of the hospital room or is walking away from the room, it means that the problem is solved and all will return to normal. If the nurse is preoccupied in treating the patient, it indicates that more work is needed on this problem and it won't be solved quickly.

Octopus

Dreams about an octopus mean that you are getting tangled up in a problem. If the octopus is grabbing you, someone around you is being too clingy and you are feeling trapped. If you are the octopus, you are being too controlling and clingy with other people, which will drive them away. If the octopus is swimming around you and releases its ink, it means that the situation you are dreaming about is cloudy and unclear and will not be easily revealed to you.

Owl

The owl is one of the most magical symbols to receive in a dream. It has the ability to see at night, which represents seeing psychically through the veil to the spirit world. It brings esoteric wisdom and practical magic to you. If the owl acts as your guide in the dream, you will soon open to your psychic abilities and your higher self/superconsciousness.

Party

To dream about going to a party indicates that you are open to more socializing. Pay attention to what type of party it is, how you feel at the party, and how others treat you at the party. If you are throwing the party in your dream, this indicates that you have greater self-confidence and are feeling good about yourself.

Phone

Many times, when loved ones who have crossed over to the other side want to come to us in a dream, they will come through by talking to us on a phone. Pay attention to this dream because it may be a visitation.

Police

Dreams about the police symbolize authority figures in your life, how you feel about authority, and if you feel respected. If you are talking to a police officer or if they are protecting you, it indicates that help will be provided for you when you need it.

If you are arguing with the police or being arrested, it indicates that you are experiencing some inner turmoil and confusion about the direction that your life is going. The police officer symbolizes the part of your consciousness that is trying to show you that you are heading in the wrong direction.

Popcorn

Popcorn in a dream is such a fun symbol, as it means that new and exciting ideas are popping up all around you and that they will be easily accessible to you for the taking. These could be creative thoughts, new opportunities, a new relationship, and even gifts from others. You are in a wonderful time in your life and should take advantage of all the opportunities and positive potential around you.

Pregnancy

Dreaming about being pregnant usually has nothing to do with being pregnant. The dream is about a part of yourself that is growing and evolving. You are about to embark on a new journey with a great new idea or project.

If you are already pregnant in real life and you dream about your pregnancy, it is one of the daily life dreams in which you are working out your thoughts and emotions about having a baby.

See the entry for baby to learn about symbolism of a future pregnancy.

Purse

In your dream, your purse or wallet indicates who you are, how you identify yourself, and how healthy your cash flow is. If you lose your wallet or purse in a dream, it indicates that you have a fear of losing who you are or how people identify you. If your wallet or purse is full of money, it indicates success and prosperity coming your way. If you dream of buying a new wallet or purse, it means that you are close to achieving your goal and that money will soon follow to reward you for your efforts.

Queen

If you are a woman and you dream of being a queen, it indicates that you are stepping into your power in the divine feminine energy. You have moved on from the princess realm, which indicates a person who has more of a desire to be pampered and spoiled. A queen takes control of her life and her destiny. If you dream about a queen who is not treating you nicely, a woman that you see as having authority over you is about to cause some conflict in your life.

If you are a man and you dream about your partner becoming a queen, it means that you recognize and respect their position in your life as your equal partner. This woman is strong, independent, loving, and powerful, and you find all these qualities attractive and engaging in your relationship.

Rain

Like so many symbols, seeing rain in a dream can mean a variety of things depending upon the intensity. Is it pouring down and storming, or is it a gentle falling rain? Depending upon what else is occurring in your dream, it can indicate your emotional well-being. If you are dreaming about something sad and it's raining, this represents your tears and grief.

If it's raining and you are outside walking in the rain or watching the rain through a window while you are working, it means that new ideas are coming to you. You are receiving a gift of inspiration that will rain down upon you soon.

CRoad

To dream about a long road ahead indicates that you are about to embark on a journey. Sometimes it can indicate travel and a road trip, and sometimes it symbolizes the long journey ahead in the new direction you are heading in your life. Pay attention to whether you are driving the car and taking control of the journey or whether you are a passenger in the car and being taken along for the ride by another person. If you are on a motorcycle, you are longing to be freed from your responsibilities in life. If you are on a bus, you are not sure where this road will take you and have felt a need to escape.

School

You may dream about your classroom if you are in school. If this is the case, you are processing your daily life thoughts in your dreams. If you are out of school, dreaming that you are back in school indicates that there is a learning curve coming in your life or career. When people dream about being naked in dreams, many times they are in a classroom environment where they are being asked to speak in front of the class. Being naked in this case represents feeling vulnerable and unsure about your situation.

Snake

Snakes are a common dream symbol. Unlike to most people's reactions to them, they actually symbolize wisdom. If you are not afraid of a snake in the dream and you pick it up, you are opening your kundalini and chakras and will have an enlightening spiritual experience. If you are not afraid of the snake and it moves toward you to climb up your leg, you are about to have a powerful sexual-awakening experience.

If you are afraid of the snake and it bites you, someone is going to cause you harm, so pay attention to whether the bite is poisonous or not so that you know how badly this person will hurt you. If a snake sheds its skin in the dream or you see a snakeskin, it indicates that a spiritual transformation is coming your way.

Sunrise

To dream about a situation that occurs during sunrise means that it is a new experience and that it will be hopeful and promising. It also indicates that younger people may be involved in this endeavor.

Sunset

To dream about an experience during sunset means that you have achieved the wisdom and knowledge from this experience, and it is now intrinsically part of you. You have grown with the wisdom of this experience and are better for having done so.

Tree

Trees indicate communication and that a message will be delivered to you soon. If the roots are predominant, the message will come from your family and will have to do with your past. If the trunk of the tree is what you notice the most, the message will have to do with your personal well-being. If the dream is focused on the branches, it indicates news about something in the future and will come from friends and acquaintances. This news may have to do with your children and other family members and friends. The condition, size, color, and shape of the tree and the color and condition of the leaves all give clues to what is going on with the message. Consult a dream encyclopedia to see the meaning of a specific type of tree.

Tornado

A dream about a tornado can be a prophetic dream, especially if it recurs several nights in a row. If a tornado appears in your dream out of the blue and moves quickly past you without causing you any harm, it means that a chaotic experience is coming your way, but it's not meant for you and you will not be directly affected during this situation. If the tornado picks you up or destroys your property, it can indicate that bad news that is going to shake you up and potentially be devastating is coming your way.

Turtle

Turtles indicate home and the state of the world. Notice the turtle in the dream. Is he calm and happy, sunning himself on a log in the lake? Or is he tense and pulling into his shell? Then notice what else is occurring in the dream around the turtle. How the turtle is reacting to his environment will give you clues to what's going on in your world and in the global consciousness of the world. Turtles can also appear in your dream to remind you to slow down and take it one step at a time. They are usually positive signs of loyalty and safety.

UFO

To dream about a UFO can mean that you are feeling alienated by the other people in your life, if the dream is not a good one. If it's exciting to get on the UFO and take off, it indicates that you are opening up to a new spiritual journey. A dream about a UFO is different from dreaming about an alien invasion, alien visitation, or abduction. Consult a dream book that deals specifically with alien dreams and experiences to understand this on a deeper level.

Vampire

If you dream of a sexy vampire who is seducing you and you are a willing participant, it implies that you are opening sexually and ready to meet someone new and to be seduced by them in one way or another.

If the vampire is scary to you in your dream and you are afraid of it attacking you, it is a warning that someone around you is wearing you out and sucking all your energy. In this case, look for clues in the dream that give hints as to whom this person could be.

Wallet

See Purse.

Water

It is very important to take notice of water in a dream. Overall, it indicates your emotional well-being. If the water is stormy and choppy, you are not feeling calm and relaxed.

The depth of the water indicates how deep the emotions are regarding the situation, so seeing water in a puddle is quite different from seeing the ocean or dreaming of a flood. Lakes can indicate a time for introspection, while oceans hint at new experiences and travel abroad.

If you're swimming in the water and feeling strong, that indicates that you'll handle what is coming your way easily. If instead you sink to the bottom, it implies that you will feel overwhelmed by the intensity of your emotions when this experience comes.

Wedding

To dream about a wedding means that something new is coming into your life. If you dream that you are getting married, pay attention to how you feel about this situation. Are you happy and excited or feeling trapped with a sense of dread? If you are engaged in real life and having bad dreams about your wedding, most times that's just stress, and you are working out all your worries and concerns about planning the wedding in your subconscious through your dreams.

If you are a guest at a wedding, notice how you feel to be there. If you are happy to be at the wedding, then you are open to something new coming your way. If you are not happy to be attending the wedding, then you are not happy with your life as it is currently. If you dream that you are wearing a wedding dress, but you are not currently engaged, you are thinking hard about the status of your current relationship and where that relationship is heading.

Whale

To dream about a whale is often a sign that you are reaching out to explore the akashic records on the spiritual planes. These are the records of all your lifetimes that are stored in the spirit world. The whale is a guide to your records and is asking if you would like to understand your karmic destiny and why you are experiencing things the way you are in this lifetime. The whale appears not just to explain this to you, but also to encourage you to step forward and share who you are with the world.

Wind

In dreams about the wind, just like with water, what matters is the strength of the wind around you. A gentle breeze in a dream indicates that spirit is around you and watching over you. Stormy winds like tornadoes or high winds indicate that chaos is coming your way. The wind blowing through your hair means you are opening up and feeling free. A howling wind is delivering upsetting news. A hurricane means your mental and emotional fields will be cleansed and cleared. A strong wind at sea means a good day for information to travel quickly. If a soft wind blows in around you, changes for the better are soon on the way. If you can control the wind in your dreams, you have achieved mastery over your thoughts and emotions.

X-Ray

If you are choosing to have an x-ray in your dream, you are actively seeking to understand a problem at a deeper level. If you are having an x-ray done and this is a surprise to you, someone around you is hiding something from you, and you will need to look deeper to find out what is truly going on.

Zombie

To dream about being eaten by zombies means that you feel that life is completely out of control and beyond what you can do to fix it. This is why zombie movies are so popular right now—people feel that the world is going completely mad and they are powerless to stop what's happening. To dream that you have become a zombie indicates that you are detaching emotionally and physically from the world and no longer want to handle stressful situations. To dream of someone you know who has become a zombie indicates that you no longer feel a connection to them. Dreams about zombies mean that you are feeling very stressed and helpless. It can be helpful to reach out to a counselor or therapist to discuss these feelings.

Bibliography

Aquinas, Thomas. *Summa Theologica.* Translated by the Fathers of the English Dominican Province. New York: Bezinger Bros., 1947. Electronic reproduction by the Internet Sacred Text Archive. http://www.sacred-texts.com /chr/aquinas/summa/.

Brenner, Charles B., and Jeffrey M. Zacks. "Why Walking through a Doorway Makes You Forget." *Scientific American*, December 13, 2011. http://www.scientificamerican .com/article/why-walking-through-doorway-makes-you -forget/.

Cayce, Edgar. *Dreams and Visions.* Virginia Beach, VA: A.R.E. Press, 2009.

Evans-Wentz, W. Y., ed. *Tibetan Yoga and Secret Doctrines: Seven Books of Wisdom of the Great Path, According to the Late Lama Kazi Dawa-Samdup's English Rendering.* 3rd ed. Oxford: Oxford University Press, 2000.

Fortune, Dion. *The Demon Lover.* Rev. ed. Newburyport, MA: Weiser, 2010.

Hegarty, Stephanie. "The Myth of the Eight-Hour Sleep." *BBC News Magazine*, February 22, 2012. http://www.bbc .com/news/magazine-16964783.

Keeney, Bradford. *Shaking Medicine: The Healing Power of Ecstatic Movement*. Rochester, VA: Destiny Books, 2007.

Leadbeater, Charles W., and Annie Besant. *Thought-Forms*. N.p., IndoEuropean Publishing, 2012.

McNamara, Patrick. "Psychopharmacology of REM Sleep and Dreams." *Psychology Today*, December 4, 2011. https://www.psychologytoday.com/blog/dream-catcher/201112/psychopharmacology-rem-sleep-and-dreams.

Pocs, Eva. *Between the Living and the Dead: A Perspective on Witches and Seers in the Early Modern Age*. Budapest: Central European University Press, 1998.

Radvansky, Gabriel, Sabine A. Krawietz, and Andrea K. Tamplin. "Walking through Doorways Causes Forgetting: Further Exploration." *The Quarterly Journal of Experimental Psychology* 64, no. 8 (2011): 1632–45. doi:10.1080/17470218.2011.571267.

Rinpoche, Tenzin Wangyal. *The Tibetan Yogas of Dream and Sleep*. Ithaca, NY: Snow Lion Publications, 1998.

To Write to the Author

If you wish to contact the author or would like more information about this book, please write to the author in care of Llewellyn Worldwide Ltd., and we will forward your request. Both the author and publisher appreciate hearing from you and learning of your enjoyment of this book and how it has helped you. Llewellyn Worldwide Ltd. cannot guarantee that every letter written to the author can be answered, but all will be forwarded. Please write to:

Kala Ambrose
℅ Llewellyn Worldwide
2143 Wooddale Drive
Woodbury, MN 55125-2989

Please enclose a self-addressed stamped envelope for reply,
or $1.00 to cover costs. If outside the USA, enclose
an international postal reply coupon.

Many of Llewellyn's authors have websites with additional information and resources. For more information, please visit our website at http://www.llewellyn.com.

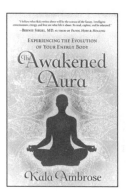

The Awakened Aura
Experiencing the Evolution of Your Energy Body
KALA AMBROSE

Humanity is entering a new era—we are evolving into super-powered beings of light. Our auric and etheric bodies are experiencing a transformational shift as new crystalline structures form within and around our auras. Kala Ambrose, a powerful wisdom teacher, intuitive, and oracle, teaches how to connect with your rapidly changing energy body to expand your awareness and capabilities on the physical, mental, emotional, and spiritual levels.

This book contains a wealth of practical exercises, diagrams, and instructions. Learn how to interpret and work with the auras of others, sense energy in animals, and sense and balance the energy in buildings and natural locations. Discover how energy cords attach in relationships, how to access the akashic records through the auric layers, how to use elemental energy to enhance your auric field, and much more.

9-780-7387-2759-2, 240 pp., 6 x 9   **$14.95**
